how to be a better....

teambuilder

Rupert Eales-White

KOGAN PAGE

The Industrial Society

HOW TO BE A BETTER... SERIES

Whether you are in a management position or aspiring to one, you are no doubt aware of the increasing need for self-improvement across a wide range of skills.

In recognition of this and sharing their commitment to management development at all levels, Kogan Page and the Industrial Society have joined forces to publish the How to be a Better... series.

Designed specifically with your needs in mind, the series covers all the core skills you need to make your mark as a high-performing and effective manager.

Enhanced by mini case studies and step-by-step guidance, the books in the series are written by acknowledged experts who impart their advice in a particular way which encourages effective action.

Now you can bring your management skills up to scratch *and* give your career prospects a boost with the How to be a Better... series!

Titles available are:
How to be Better at Giving Presentations
How to be a Better Problem Solver
How to be a Better Interviewer
How to be a Better Teambuilder
How to be Better at Motivating People
How to be a Better Decision Maker

Forthcoming titles are:
How to be a Better Negotiator
How to be a Better Project Manager
How to be a Better Creative Thinker
How to be a Better Communicator

Available from all good booksellers. For further information on the series, please contact:
Kogan Page
120 Pentonville Road
London N1 9JN
Tel: 0171 278 0433
Fax: 0171 837 6348

THE INDUSTRIAL SOCIETY

The Industrial Society stands for changing people's lives. In nearly eighty years of business, the Society has a unique record of transforming organisations by unlocking the potential of their people, bringing unswerving commitment to best practice and tempered by a mission to listen and learn from experience.

The Industrial Society's clear vision of ethics, excellence and learning at work has never been more important. Over 10,000 organisations, including most of the companies that are household names, benefit from corporate Society membership.

The Society works with these and non-member organisations, in a variety of ways – consultancy, management and skills training, in-house and public courses, information services and multi-media publishing. All this with the single vision – to unlock the potential of people and organisations by promoting ethical standards, excellence and learning at work.

If you would like to know more about the Industrial Society please contact us.

The Industrial Society
48 Bryanston Square
London
W1H 7LN
Telephone 0171 262 2401

The Industrial Society is a Registered Charity No. 290003

If you would like to obtain more information from the author on the techniques described in this book, please contact him directly on: +44 (0)181-313-7473.

First published in 1996, reprinted 1997 (twice), 1998

Kogan Page Limited
120 Pentonville Road
London N1 9JN

British Library Cataloguing in Publication Data

A CIP record for this book is available from the British Library.

ISBN 0 7494 1912 1

Typeset by DP Photosetting, Aylesbury, Bucks
Printed in England by Clays Ltd, St Ives plc

CONTENTS

PREFACE

PURPOSE

The purpose of this book is to help you become a better team-builder in the workplace. In fact, the goal is to enable you to build an effective team, where the outputs are superior in quality and quantity than the combination of purely individual efforts – referred to as a synergistic team.

Effective teams are quite rare in the workplace, and if you have been a member of such a team, you will know that they are very special – they are a joy to be a part of and are the most powerful learning vehicle for each individual team member. Effective teams are not difficult to build, and require four things: belief, knowledge, techniques, and their application to your team to develop skill.

Belief

This book cannot create belief in teams, but will certainly encourage it. The fact that you are reading it provides a strong base – commitment and the willingness to learn.

Knowledge

The book will provide you with in-depth knowledge of how to build a team. We all develop knowledge of how to do our jobs, and many of us are skilled professionals, with qualifications gained by years of study, reinforced by experience and technical training in our jobs.

Few of us develop knowledge about teams, because however important our organisations may rate teamwork and team leadership (and you just need to scan the job adverts, and teamwork is invariably mentioned), there has been a failure to recognise that knowledge about teamwork should be provided to staff, not just knowledge about how to carry out the tasks we need to complete.

For instance, when a team-member is replaced, the effective team builder (ETB) needs to go back to basics, and build *as if all the team members were new*. Not knowing that (and the reasons will be explained in Chapter 7) can delay or deny team performance in the future.

Effective leadership of individuals is predicated on self-awareness, self-belief and self-respect. Those realities hold for team leadership.

We are all more able than we think we are. We all have latent potential, yet to be released. This book will help you recognise your abilities and release and harness your potential as an ETB.

Techniques

The book covers the key techniques required to build a team: how to promote discovery through effective questioning and listening, what processes to apply and how, and how to manage the flow of ideas to achieve optimal solutions to problems.

Application

Skill comes from the application of knowledge and techniques to the real world – the world of experience. You have the goal of building an effective team. The book helps you apply the learning progressively to build your team. In fact, there is an exercise, at the end of Chapter 2, in which you should involve your team as a special event. It will be a very positive and powerful experience, and will create a strong base for effective teamworking.

In Chapter 5 there is a questionnaire, which you and all your team members should fill in to gather data on the mix of skills in your team, and in the final chapter, there is space for you to complete an action plan to become a better teambuilder.

The suggestion is that, apart from the special exercise, or gathering data about the team, you should not begin the process of building your team until you have completed your action plan.

One of the hallmarks of an effective team is that the members think and plan together before effective action. That is just as true for the individual ETB.

CONTENT

There are eight chapters, and Chapter 1 introduces the key themes to be explored in the rest of the book. Chapter 2 answers the question 'why build a team?', and considers the difference between an effective team and an interacting group. Too often, when building teams, we use the task as the sole motivator, not realising that we can motivate through developing a shared vision of the team destination – the effective team we will have built.

We also explore some of the key barriers to effective team-working and how they can be overcome, and conclude with the exercise that will enable you to produce synergy in your own team.

Chapter 3 looks at the key skills of effective questioning, listening and creative thinking, and concludes with the pivotal technique of effective brainstorming.

Chapter 4 looks at the stages or levels of individual development and then transfers the individual case to the group situation, examining the different stages or phases that groups go through before operating effectively, and what you, as ETB, can do to accelerate progress to peak performance.

Chapter 5 is a very practical chapter where you can identify and evaluate all the strengths each team member brings to the team, and consider such issues as where strength duplication might lead to 'personality' clashes, and where a strength is absent and needs developing to avoid imperfect team performance.

Chapter 6 considers the processes involved to develop the team and complete the team tasks, and Chapter 7 considers how individuals react to change and how the team and the team-builder can cope with all the changes that can and will occur.

Chapter 8 summarises the key messages of the earlier chapters, as well as enabling you to develop an action plan to be a better teambuilder.

I wish you every joy on your personal voyage of discovery, and every success in achieving what is one of the greatest skills a manager can have – becoming a better teambuilder and building an effective team.

Rupert Eales-White

VOYAGE OF DISCOVERY

INTRODUCTION

In this chapter, we introduce the key themes that we will need to explore together to enable you to develop the confidence and competence to be a better teambuilder, and hence build an effective team in the workplace.

We do so by looking at a particular situation that a number of groups of managers have faced, and conclude with a case study.

THE IMMATURE GROUP

Just imagine that you and five of your colleagues from work have been magically transported to the middle of a grassy glade in a sunlit wood in the height of summer. You have all agreed to complete some tasks, which will help you learn how to be more effective as team members.

You have completed a few warm-up exercises to get used to the new environment and are being introduced to the first task, which you and your colleagues have to complete in 30 minutes.

You have been asked to put on blindfolds, and are still recovering from the shock of having to work in the dark, literally, when the instructor throws some equipment into the middle of the group of six, and utters this statement: '*With the equipment provided, form a perfect square, and place yourselves equidistant around it.*'

Can you guess how you would be all be feeling, and what happens next?

Let us consider an actual example, which is the way nearly all groups of managers behave, even when they have received guidance as to how to operate successfully in a group.

As you will appreciate, there is a lot of uncertainty and discomfort. When operating in such an environment, we want answers. We want to remove the uncertainty and gain a little bit of security, as quickly as we can.

The individuals in the group rush to find out what the equipment actually is, with a few near misses when it comes to the bumping of heads. The equipment is a very long piece of rope, say 20 metres, neatly curled up.

The pattern of behaviour and action are as follows.

❑ To begin with and for some considerable time, there is maximum heat and minimum light – a number of the group talk at each other, without listening – vying for the leadership. Helpful suggestions by other group members like 'Shall we nominate one person to co-ordinate our efforts' or 'let's not implement one idea, before we have explored all the options' are completely lost in the noise.

❑ The individual who can get the group to listen to his or her idea first becomes the leader – but leadership follows the development of the idea, changing when someone else modifies the idea or takes over the implementation.

❑ There comes a time when the majority are locked into one solution, and any alternative put forward is dismissed out of hand.

❑ Clarity of communication is poor because of the over-reliance on words (though the amount of unseen gesticulation is very high!), and towards the end, people are doing what they have been told to do by the task leader, quite cheerfully but badly, with little understanding of what they are actually doing and why.

❑ In the middle phase, there is subgrouping with no cross-communication. Additionally, there are one or two individuals completely turned off, just standing holding the rope, waiting morosely for something to happen.

❑ Once everyone has got hold of a bit of the rope, there is

considerable reluctance to let it go. Indeed, in many groups, only solutions which permit continuous holding of the rope by all members are implemented.

❑ In most groups, the standard solution involves full use of the rope with an attempt to produce an enormous square.

❑ Individuals can become quite dogmatic, not only locking into the 'one right answer', but also into a completely wrong answer. For instance, one individual in one group asserted strongly that there were two ropes. This was accepted by the group as a whole and a solution developed and implemented until the evidence against the proposition became overwhelming.

❑ Most solutions involve activity by all towards the end. Then, individuals begin to believe they will succeed, energy levels and commitment soar, and the end comes much more quickly than external observers anticipate. It is as if 90 per cent of the time is spent in confusion and muddle, and almost magically a result is achieved right at the end.

❑ Some groups never make it, but those that do, before they take off their blindfold, are very satisfied with the outcome. For most groups, that satisfaction is diminished when they see a very imperfect square or there has been no attempt to place themselves 'equidistant around it', as everyone forgot that part of the brief.

Although lack of sight exaggerates our behaviours, managers recognise that what happens in this exercise is a fair reflection of behaviours and actions that unformed teams or immature groups exhibit at work. We will look at this in more detail in Chapter 4.

THE EFFECTIVE TEAM

Now we look at success: how an effective team would tackle this exercise, where you are the effective teambuilder (ETB), and you have George, Alice, Mark, Zainol and Lucia to help. The starting point is the same – you have all received the instruction: *'With the equipment provided, form a perfect square, and place yourselves equidistant around it.'*

ETB (with considerable authority):
   'Now team, before we do anything, let us make sure we all understand the brief. Alice, can you remember what the instructor just said?'

Alice: 'Well, er, I think he said that "with the equipment provided, form a perfect square".'

ETB: 'Thanks, Alice – was that all?'

Zainol: 'No, I don't think so. Didn't he also say that when we have formed a perfect square with the equipment provided, we should place ourselves equidistant around it.'

ETB: 'Well done, Zainol. You're right. George, would you mind summarising it for all of us, so that we all know exactly what we have to achieve.'

George: 'With the equipment provided, we have to form a perfect square, and then place ourselves equidistant around it.'

ETB: 'Excellent. Now we all know what we have to do, we need to find out what this "equipment provided" is precisely. Lucia and Zainol, could you both kneel down, investigate and when you both agree, tell us what you find.'

A minute goes by.

Lucia: 'It's a long piece of rope – just a single rope and it is difficult to measure precisely – but it must be around 20 metres, as it is 20 of Zainol's arm lengths.'

ETB: 'Thank you, Lucia and Zainol. We know what we have to do, and we now know what the equipment is. Let us put our thinking hats on and question the brief – in case we are making unnecessary assumptions, which will reduce the quality of the solution. "Form a perfect square with the long rope provided and place ourselves equidistant around it." Any questions on the brief?'

Pause.

Mark: 'I have had a thought – do we need to use all the rope to form the square – couldn't we use just a small portion and then place ourselves around that – much easier than trying to form a very large square?'

ETB: 'That's an interesting idea. It doesn't say "all the rope" in the brief. What do the others think?'
General agreement ensues.
ETB: 'Good, so the next questions are how to form a small square and how to place ourselves equidistant around it.'

I will not continue the conversation through to the end, as we have glimpsed enough to see an ETB in operation. Within less than ten minutes, blindfolds were removed to display a team of six people with arms linked (not hands with variable length of arms) around a neat little square of rope. This result has happened but once during my involvement with this exercise. You should have heard the cry of triumph that went up, when they saw the result they instinctively knew they had achieved before sight was restored.

KEY THEMES

Taking the two situations we have described, we can identify key themes, which we will develop in the rest of the book.

Power of process

Now the ETB is very much in charge, but not of the individuals of the team. The ETB does not tell the individuals in the team what to do. The leadership approach is focused on getting results through the individuals in the team. To do this, the ETB follows a defined process – separating out task achievement into a series of steps, each in its appointed place. Chapter 6 looks at the different processes involved in building a team. Figure 1.1 summarises an initial process, when an ETB is using the team to complete a known task.

Promoting discovery

An effective team is a very powerful development tool for each individual member, including you, the ETB. As the team grows, so do the individuals. In fact, a team is not fully effective unless

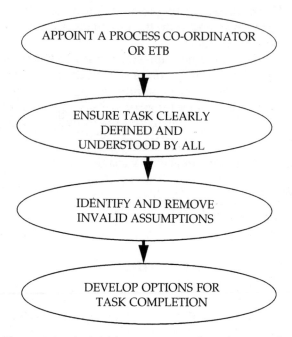

Figure 1.1 *An initial process to complete a known task*

the individuals have developed with the team. As mentioned, the stages that groups go through are covered in Chapter 4. What an effective team looks like, what it can achieve and how it achieves it is covered in Chapter 2.

An ETB needs to have or develop first class questioning and listening skills (evidenced in the success story), as well as managing successfully the key teambuilding technique, known commonly as 'brainstorming', ie managing the generation of ideas in that phase of the process.

These skills and the technique are covered in Chapter 3.

Playing to strength

When building an effective team, it is vital that, in the early stages, individuals play to their strengths, and are not asked to overcome weaknesses. The reason is that individuals need to develop confidence and competence, which come from strength recognition and application. Chapter 5 enables strengths to be determined for all team-members, including you – the team-builder. It is when a team is moving towards strong performance that review mechanisms can be introduced, individuals encouraged to develop a broader range of skills than their current base, and the full power of the team and the individual unleashed.

Dealing with change

When groups of managers put on blindfolds and are presented with an unclear task, they face an unexpected change. Part of the reason for subsequent poor performance is reaction to such sudden change. Teams face changes all the time, whether it is in reaching their goals as an intact team, or as the result of changes to the composition of the team itself.

All key changes and how the ETB can respond to maximum effect are covered in Chapter 7.

The final chapter reviews the key points from earlier chapters.

To conclude this chapter, we reinforce these key themes by considering a case study.

CASE STUDY

The story is told in the words of the ETB, Glyn Murphy. The key messages are in italics.

In the early 1990s, I joined a Health Authority Learning Disabilities Team, in a deprived inner city area, as clinical psychologist and team co-ordinator. The team had originally been set up some six years previously, when its main task had been to resettle people with learning disabilities from the large, local mental handicap hospital, which was closing. Since then, all had been settled in the community and many had then required support, so the team had to adapt itself to provide them with new community-based services.

Originally, team-members had been heavily involved in ensuring that the community-based (Health Service) group homes, where most of the people went to live, were properly run and managed but, just before my arrival, these houses were transferred to a housing consortium, out of the Health Authority's purview, since they were construed as providing largely 'social care' as opposed to 'health care'.

The team, therefore, had had to adjust to a number of new roles over a brief period.

The team included physiotherapists, occupational therapists, psychologists, a community nurse, a speech therapist, a psychiatrist and a secretary, with the more senior people supervising the more junior ones.

It was clear that our first task needed to be some teambuilding and shortly after I arrived we all debated what form this should take.

There was general agreement that we should involve all team members and that we would need at least two days. There was also a unanimous feeling that the two days needed to be off-site, so that we were not disturbed by constant phone calls and pleas for help from desperate social workers or clients.

The team days were a great success, but were also task-oriented.

We decided we wanted to tackle the real problems the team faced, rather than having an event to bond the team, which was unrelated to our pressing problems.

We began the first morning by *brainstorming* the topic areas we wanted to consider, then refining this list down to a manageable size. In the afternoon, we split into three smaller groups, each taking one topic, brainstorming the problems in the area and possible solutions, and aiming to come up with the best solutions by the end of the afternoon.

This process was repeated the next morning with other topics in different sub-groups and we ended in the afternoon by feeding back to each other all our deliberations and deciding what we should take forward.

At the end of those two days, we felt we had a common purpose, we knew what our purpose was, and we had ambitions about how to achieve our goals.

Much of our day-to-day work with people with learning disabilities was done by individuals from the team working alone with the client and the client carers, although where clients had multiple, complex difficulties, several team members would work together.

This meant that sharing our work experiences in the weekly team meeting, in giving brief client updates, was extremely important, since we could both inform our colleagues about progress with clients and ask them for ideas if we were stuck.

Much informal support between team members also took place at these meetings and the support took many forms, from comparing the frustrations of working with certain staff teams in some of the community-based homes to offering joint visiting to a client who was living alone, and becoming aggressive and threatening when visited. We had, of course, somewhat different skills to offer, according to our training, but also had many common practices and areas of overlap, *so that joint working was seen as a pleasure rather than a threat.*

One essential aspect of working in such a team though, was respect for other team members' professional knowledge and skill.

Some of that respect was gained in our weekly meetings when we reviewed work with clients over the previous year and set plans for the next year. At such times, we heard our colleagues describe what they had achieved or tried to achieve for clients, sometimes over years of working.

There were many stresses for team members, as we were working in a very deprived area of a big city and often had to visit clients in large run-down estates; we would often see families coping against enormous odds and with little help from an over-stretched social services department; we would sometimes be shouted and screamed at or hit by our clients or have objects thrown at us; we would spend months setting up special programmes for clients only to see their staff unwilling to make the effort to carry them out.

So from time to time, we decided we had earned some fun and we would have a team outing to the local bowling-alley or a meal together in a restaurant.

In our team, there was no real hierarchical head, no 'boss man' (or woman) who told people what to do.

I was merely the co-ordinator and my most important duty was, as I saw it, bringing out team members' strengths, pulling out their best ideas and setting up ways in which those could be put into practice.

In many ways we were like a family: we had junior members and senior members, people with different skills and interests, and my job was to get the whole team to work together. We were certainly not all alike; some of us were extremely careful and well-organised, some were disorganised but had brilliant ideas; some were extroverts, some were very sociable, some less so.

They simply needed nurturing.

One of our difficulties was that we did not feel we needed managing from above.

We were trying to survive, however, in a rapidly changing Health Service, where the pace of change was sometimes so fast that people felt shell-shocked. Perhaps we should have seen what was on the horizon. We woke up one day to find out that, as a result of a minor sub-paragraph in a government-sponsored report on the Health Service in our area, we were to be split off from our parent organisation, divided and sent to bolster up two other teams in neighbouring areas.

There was no consultation with us (we were told this was contingency management), no discussion, no clear decisions, just muddle and confusion, followed by reallocation.

I felt bereaved for months.

I have highlighted the key points – and do not intend to go into detailed analysis. The words speak for themselves. However, there are one or two points, which can usefully be made to conclude this first chapter:

❏ Effective teams agree vision, mission and strategy as a team. Implementation is necessarily carried out on an individual or sub-group basis. Regular team communication ensures the sharing of experience and team support to solve individual problems.
❏ Change produces uncertainty and discomfort. Individuals need to develop a sense of direction and purpose to regain some of the comfort that change, if imposed, necessarily destroys. The climate was right.
❏ Glyn was the type of ETB they needed. She had a clear view of her role as a co-ordinator of process and not a controller of people.
❏ Effective brainstorming is the pivotal technique to build the team and achieve the task.
❏ Effective teams become self-managing units. This imposes a duty of care on decision-takers higher up in the organisation and the recognition that the team needs freedom to breathe in order to do more demanding and different work than his-

torically the case. Where possible, the ETB needs to try to educate these decision-makers on the back of significantly improved performance.

THE EFFECTIVE TEAM

INTRODUCTION

In this chapter, we consider answers to the questions: why build a team, what does an effective team actually look like, what are the barriers to achieving success and how can they be overcome? We conclude the chapter with practical exercise, which you can use with your team to demonstrate how easy it is to build an effective team.

WHY BUILD A TEAM?

We look at organisational reasons and individual reasons.

Organisational

There are many research findings from many countries on the benefits of teamworking. As Anthony Montebello and Victor Buzzotta wrote in an article 'Work teams that work': 'Companies that are willing to rethink old ways and develop teams can profit by increasing quality and productivity. And they can develop a workforce that is motivated and committed.'

An American Society of Training and Development HRD (Human Resource Development) Executives received responses from 230 HRD executives about teamwork results. The survey found that:

❏ Productivity improved in 77 per cent of the respondents' companies.
❏ Quality improvements due to teamwork were reported in 72 per cent of companies.
❏ Waste was reduced in 55 per cent of firms.
❏ Job satisfaction improved in 65 per cent of the companies.
❏ Customer satisfaction improved in 55 per cent of companies.

Additional benefits cited were more efficient production scheduling, improved production goal-setting and increased ability of team members to resolve their own disputes.

Quoting Tom Peters from his book: *Thriving on Chaos: Handbook for a Management Revolution*

> *I observe the power of the team is so great that it is often wise to violate common sense and force a team structure on almost anything ... companies that do will achieve a greater focus, stronger task orientation, more innovation and enhanced individual commitment.*

However, if we look at the reverse side of the research findings quoted:

❏ 23 per cent of companies saw no increase in productivity.
❏ 28 per cent did not enjoy quality improvements from team-working.
❏ 45 per cent did not reduce waste.
❏ There was no improvement in job satisfaction for 35 per cent.
❏ 45 per cent saw no increase in customer satisfaction.

What the research does not indicate is the extent to which effective teams were developed. The more the teams remained immature groups, as in the blindfold squares exercise, the less the benefit derived from a team approach.

Individual

Quoting the managing director of a glass manufacturing company, who had recruited a senior manager with the specific role of building an effective team:

> *Keith (the senior manager) really does understand what motivates people and has this unique ability actually to bring the best out of*

people. I think he gets people to perform better than their own individual expectations.

We have seen our production costs go down, we have seen new products being introduced, using different manufacturing techniques, which were not available before, we've seen investment in the business better identified to help manufacturing efficiency, so there's a whole list of things you can see coming from the efforts of those people, who, other than Keith, were the same people that we had before. We have got a far greater output from them and the company has benefited.

ETBs like Keith and Glyn are not unique. We all have an ETB lurking within us. By changing the environment, by allowing people to ask questions and discover answers, by building trust and mutual respect, ETBs enable the same people to achieve more than they thought possible.

The effective team is the most powerful development tool for all the individual team members, including the ETB!

WHAT DOES AN EFFECTIVE TEAM LOOK LIKE?

We have been talking a lot about the effective team – but what exactly does an effective team look like, and, why is it important that you and all your team members know this early on in the teambuilding or team improvement process?

Dealing with the latter first, you cannot have escaped noticing how most organisations have or are going through a process to determine their *vision* for their future and the *values* required to achieve it. This is perceived as necessary, given accelerating change and uncertainty in external business environments. It can be effective, if the process of determining vision and values is a shared one and the values propagated are lived by the leaders who propagate them, *and* there is structural and system change that ensures alignment with the vision and values.

For instance, if, as is the case with quite a few organisations, one of the core values is, in fact, teamworking, and you find a rigid hierarchy, a top team that is clearly acting as an immature and political group, reward systems based purely on individuals achieving targets, and no support for leaders to develop teamworking and team-leadership skills, then the probability of success is extremely low from an organisational perspective, though individual ETBs can transcend such barriers and achieve success.

As Glyn said: 'we felt we had a common purpose, we knew what our purpose was and we had ambitions.'

That team had built a picture of the *task mission*. Teambuilding is accelerated if all team members have a picture of the *team vision* – what their team will look like and what values will be required to achieve the vision.

The reason is that having both a task mission and a team vision ensures that all know early on what is required of them and the team to achieve both. It maximises motivation and commitment, as it generates a sense of purpose both to task achievement and team development, ensuring that the team is effective in completing its work purpose.

The two processes are inextricably interlinked, and are covered in Chapter 6.

So what does an effective team look like, and what values are necessary to achieve success?

We will determine this together. It is easy, but dangerous for me, simply to say that this or that is the case. You may not believe me, as you have not been part of the process of discovery. So I would ask you to take a piece of paper and a pen, and, first of all, accentuate the negative!

Think of all the occasions that you have been with a group of work colleagues and wished you had been elsewhere! List down all the reasons that made you feel that way – what was happening or not happening that upset you, or annoyed you, or demotivated you.

When you have done that, simply reverse each of the negative factors – and you will have built a picture of an effective team!

Let us see how your experience and views compare with a group of managers who carried out the same exercise. Figure 2 .1 summarises their views and Figure 2.2 paints the reverse picture.

Figure 2.2 is a list of actions, attitudes and behaviours that comprise an effective team. It is not a traditional vision statement with specific values. If you intend to build a vision, it should be a shared activity with the team, with you leading the process. The

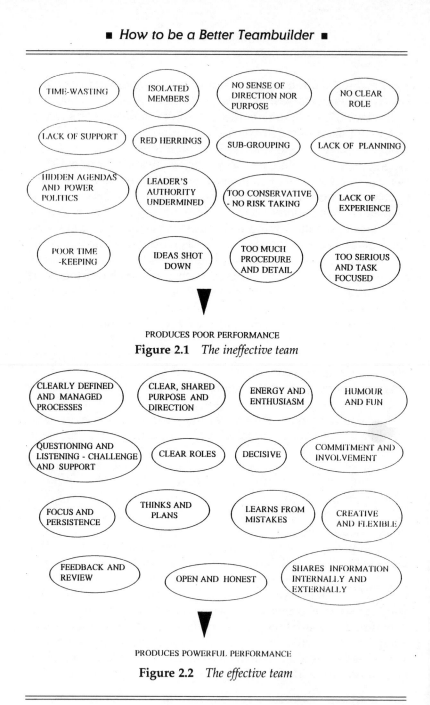

PRODUCES POOR PERFORMANCE

Figure 2.1 *The ineffective team*

PRODUCES POWERFUL PERFORMANCE

Figure 2.2 *The effective team*

end product will be your own team's vision statement and values which all believe in and will strive to follow.

However, I will put forward a summary vision and value statement to complete the picture.

Vision

Our team, when effective, will:

Have a clear, shared sense of direction and purpose, with enthusiastic, committed team members who are all involved and participate. We will focus on achieving stretching and demanding tasks and goals, supporting and helping each other develop and grow our individual strengths. We will have fun together, and be able to question and challenge each other, so that the team and the individual can continuously improve.

Values

The core values which will help us become an effective team are openness, honesty, mutual respect, trust, sharing and humour.

WHAT ARE THE BARRIERS?

Having developed a picture of what an effective team looks like, we now examine the barriers to success and how they can be overcome – separating out organisational or cultural barriers and individual barriers.

Cultural

Executive mind-set

Let us take an example. A manufacturing company, with a number of divisions operating in distinct business areas, but related fields, had a culture of individualism, competitiveness and achievement. The team as a concept was talked about. Over time, more team structures were put in place, as is the case for most companies. Some form of quality circle was introduced at the production level, with moderate success.

The top decision-makers were not believers in teamwork. There was little effective cross-fertilisation across the divisions and quite a lot of competition between them.

There were many opportunities where teamwork would have added enormous value, particularly cross-divisional project teams to achieve specific tasks, eg divisional audits to identify and promulgate best practice.

They did not happen, as the need was not perceived. If the decision-takers had believed in teams, then they would have recognised where teams were needed and deployed them to leverage the bottom line, which was king.

Belief produces motivation to search, which produces identification of needs to fill.

This is, of course, how a team culture is brought into being in the most effective way – through the leadership and strategic thinking skills of the top decision-takers, custodians of the culture, who can deny or deliver effective cultural change.

However, for many companies, lack of strategic thinking skills, combined with a focus on task, confirm cultures where teamworking as both a living reality and a cultural norm are inhibited.

Focusing on getting the job done

I learnt the impact of this from an operations director, newly appointed to a subsidiary board, but it can and does occur at all levels.

It was all based on the 'assumption of maturity' as he put it. Once he joined the board, he became part of the élite, he sat at the top table – he was a big boy now. It was assumed that he was mature, that he could handle the pressures of the big league. What this actually meant was that there was no need whatsoever to consider emotions and relationship management or, for that matter, process management. Simply get on with the job and achieve the many tasks that had to be done – collectively or individually.

Now we know that relationships and emotions need to be managed explicitly if effective teamwork is going to prevail. A focus on task will deny that for all time, and will usually result in a group operating with many of the negative attitudes, actions and behaviours we have already identified.

If the culture is 'can do', then there can be too much focus on tasks and task achievement, which denies effective teamworking.

Poor strategic thinking

Those who think strategically combine four key skills. They are able to:

Peel the onion – differentiate between cause and effect and determine core causes of a problem.

Think outside the box – break out of false paradigms, assumptions, constraints and mind-sets, and develop new perspectives, fresh insights and more effective solutions.

Cut through the detail – understand what matters and what can be ignored – being able to abstract from the detail what impacts on the tactical or strategic.

Draw out the consequences – understand the practical effects of potential decisions, and alter them through recognising the difference between theory and practice in advance. This requires the understanding of people and how they respond to different stimuli.

This is one reason why so many like Tom Peters see the team as the tool for effective change management. Individuals may well have an incomplete set of skills to be effective strategic thinkers. A team that values and deploys different individual strengths can think strategically.

Clearly, with a task focus, and with the pressures of the short term, there is often a combination of little time given to, as well as little skill deployed at, the strategic level.

The consequences are that, even where there is a belief at the top in teams, the culture may remain hostile to teams, despite cultural statements. In the case of one company, where teamworking was part of the vision and promulgated to everyone as one of the four critical success factors of the future, every employee was expected to buy into it.

In a culture that is parent/child, telling the child to believe in teams does not work!

Lack of strategic thinking means the development or continuation of key bulwarks of a non-team culture, which leads to two more key barriers, mentioned earlier.

Structure

Where there is positional power, a significant hierarchy (so that there are a number of different grades and status levels in, say, a departmental team) and downward appraisal, ie the traditional structure supporting the traditional parent/child culture, then effective teamworking is difficult.

Systems

Equally, reward systems, which are individually based, and provide positive or negative financial and non-financial rewards, depending on the achievement of quantifiable targets, encourage competition between individuals and not co-operation in groups. They also accentuate the level and pain of 'office politics'.

Impact on ETB

You know the culture of your organisation – you know, whatever the words, how positive or negative it is to teams and you face the decision as to whether you can build an effective team.

The good news is that as leader, you have enormous power. I have not yet come across any organisation where individual leaders, who have built effective teams, have not benefited in career terms. Even with cultures, where there is a rigid hierarchy, individually focused reward systems and downward appraisal, teambuilders thrive. I can recall two individuals operating in such a culture.

One focused on fixing his gaze upwards to the firmament of more senior managers, with an occasional glance sideways, and happily ignored or abused downwards.

The other, who operated with the same constraints because he worked in the same organisation at the same level (both were heads of departments), believed in teams and helped build a team atmosphere. Many of the 90 or so people who worked in his department advised me that, of all the bosses they had experienced in their working lives, he was the only one they respected *and* trusted. He had motivated them more than any other.

Five years on, he is a main board director; his colleague/rival is not.

Individual

In this section, we look at five key individual barriers to effective teamwork.

Personal

One of the key constraints is the belief, attitude, knowledge and skill of the leader himself or herself. I remember a senior manager who had been on a development programme, which had two modules. At the end of the first he stated that he was going back to build his team.

Four months later, when he returned on the second module, he advised that he no longer believed in all this 'team and empowerment rubbish', and was annoyed with us for leading him down the garden path.

He had been a strong leader, who played lip-service to involving the team in decision-taking. In other words, he made up his mind on a particular problem or issue in advance of any team meeting, called team meetings where there was 'officially' a discussion, at the end of which his unchanged view prevailed. A total waste of the team members' time of course, and the worst of both worlds. People, generally, are not stupid. They knew the game he was playing, would have been de-motivated by an artificial and pointless exercise, and, as they were never going to be involved in decision-taking, would have preferred just to be told what to do and when.

At his first meeting after the first module, he said that he was going to genuinely share decision-taking, and he would abide by the majority vote! There was a major decision required, which went to a vote, where the leader was in a minority.

A few weeks later he had to reverse the decision, as it was not working (!) and revert to his preferred choice. As he put it: 'A waste of time, a waste of money and it knocked the team back to a worse position than at the start.'

Belief alone is not sufficient. Knowing what to do, when, why, and how – this is the knowledge that this books aims to impart.

Skills

Here we consider two types of skills – technical and team. As regards the technical competence of the team as a whole, clearly there needs to be present sufficient to understand the task and the task requirements. It is not necessary to have a complete range of expertise for a task, like a project, that will take months to complete. One of the great advantages of teamwork is that it provides an opportunity for individuals to be stretched and develop. This development includes technical skills. What is required, a point developed in Chapter 6, is the identification of what technical competence needs to be developed by whom and when in order for the project to be completed successfully.

As an aside, when President Kennedy stated 'In ten years we will have a man on the moon', many technical skills were absent as the technologies had not been invented! Yet the goal was achieved.

As regards team skills, we look in detail at this in Chapter 5. Clearly if the strategic thinking skills are absent, or everyone has preference for evaluation and implementation, it will be very difficult to build an effective team, which leads to the next point.

Mix

It is important that there is the right mix of technical skill, strategic thinking skills and interpersonal skills. As developed in

Chapter 5, it is not necessary for the entire range of skills to be present, simply that any duplication (which can lead to personality clashes) or absence is identified, so that strategies can be devised and implemented to ensure the right blend and balance.

Location

The ideal situation for effective teamwork is physical co-location of the team. The more there is physical separation, the more difficult it is to build an effective team, and the harder the ETB will need to work in the areas of information sharing and goal setting. Synergy will be low, unless the leader/company is prepared to pay the cost of regular team meetings in one location.

There was a departmental manager of a large pharmaceutical company, who had three senior managers running their own teams. Two of the managers worked near him and one four miles away. He wanted to build a united, effective team of four, and went on a teambuilding experience with his three managers. Inevitably, the fourth member, who was physically absent, felt remote and isolated and jealous of the other members' easy and instant access to the boss.

The experience went some way in reducing these feelings, and improving the team performance, but it was only when they were all relocated to a new building that synergy soared.

Numbers

You cannot have an effective team if you have too many team members. The law of diminishing returns sets in. The greater the numbers, the greater the chance of 'negergy'. (Synergy is a positive word, coming from the Ancient Greek 'working together'. Negative synergy is, therefore, a nonsense combination. As there is no single word for the opposite of synergy, let us call it 'negergy'.)

The key reasons are:

1. It becomes increasingly difficult for everyone to participate, to feel involved and stay committed.
2. There is more danger of sub-groups that are independent of

rather than connected to the main group, and which may compete with each other.

3. Less chance of clear relevant task roles, which are not duplicated.

4. Duplication of skills or preferred approaches, increasing the potential for clashes.

5. The ability to sense the mood of the team and the individuals diminishes. We have limited capacity to perceive and be aware.

So what is the right number?

There is not a definite answer, as it depends on the complexity and requirements of the project, and the skill mix of the members. Most experts believe that it varies between four and eight. Certainly, in the years I have helped build effective teams, the numbers have varied from four to eight.

You can get some synergy with more, as can be seen with football teams, very occasionally! Football teams are helped by having complete clarity and lack of clash in work roles – the separate positions on the field.

You can of course produce a group atmosphere among large numbers, but that is not the same as effective teamworking.

PRACTICAL EXERCISE

Synergy is important because you, as an ETB, can create it very rapidly – in fact you can build an effective team, even if temporarily, in a remarkably short space of time.

This final section is all about how you can do so and what to do.

The fundamental difference between an effective team of individuals and a group of individuals is that a group produces 'negergy', while an effective team produces synergy. By 'negergy', I mean that the value generated collectively by the group is less than what would have been generated if the individuals had acted on their own. In fact, there is an awful lot of negergy about when groups get together. This is why so many managers have said to me that they get their best work done when on their own, either first thing in the morning, if they are early birds, or in the evening, if they are night owls.

Synergy occurs only if there is discovery in the group. In other words, the interactions of the individuals in the group lead to the development of new knowledge, insights, angles, and solutions – none of which the individuals acting on their own could have produced. In short, by the effective interaction of different individuals, value is created and applied to improve business performance.

So, if you can create an environment, where there is such discovery, you have created an effective team.

You can do so and the medium is what is termed 'lateral thinking' questions.

However, to guarantee the result, you will have to sell the exercise to your team (which can be as the first of a number of steps, which the team will consider, to build a better team) and follow the guidelines I set out.

As already discovered, we all make assumptions that limit our ability to come up with good solutions. In each question is an assumption or assumptions, that, if uncovered, will lead to a better solution. By the team, including you, uncovering these assumptions, better solutions will be developed than would otherwise be the case – there will be group discovery.

Let us take an example.

A women jumps from the top of a New York skyscraper. It is a deliberate act of suicide. As she tumbles to her death, she hears a telephone ring. She cries out 'I wish I had not jumped'. Explain her behaviour.

The first point to make is that the exercise should generate laughter and fun (producing some of the core values of an effective team). So everyone should be encouraged to come up with answers, with no criticism of those answers. Suppose someone says (if you were using this one by way of example) that she thought she was dying of cancer, and the doctor had promised to confirm the results an hour ago. She had waited and waited and then jumped. When she heard the telephone, she wished she had not, in case the news was good. Be positive about this suggestion, check what assumption is being made to produce this answer and encourage different answers. Specifically, try to focus the group on considering what assumptions are being made. All the information is, in fact, relevant, and information not provided is irrelevant.

As I have said, and you should confirm, there is no wrong answer, but better solutions are developed if someone notices the indefinite article in front of the word 'telephone'. It is 'a' telephone and not 'the' telephone. If people assume, as many do, that it is 'the' telephone, then they create stories where the caller is known to the woman. If they pick up on 'a' telephone, then they think up stories where a complete stranger has made the call. Explanations might be a 'neutron' holocaust, where the woman was convinced she was the only person left alive, and could not bear the isolation, or the more prosaic deafness she regretted the decision, when she heard a telephone ring.

The questions are set out separately on page 37, headed *Questioning Assumptions*, enabling you to photocopy them for each team member if you wish.

If it works, which it almost invariably does, you can have a short review at the end, to confirm some basic points.

There should have been humour, enjoyment and some 'silly answers' – the development of an environment with good questioning and listening skills displayed.

To the question, 'Do you feel that, if you had worked on these problems on your own, you would have done so well?', the answer from all should be that they performed better by being part of the group, confirming the discovery that is the heart of effective teamworking.

To the question, 'Did you find, on occasions, that the answer came as a flash to one individual, and not the same one, but that flash of insight or inspiration was helped by the comments and questions of other members of the group?', all should say yes, confirming how we can all be more creative than we think we are, and, again, the power of positive group interaction.

Finally, you may be asking, 'Where are the answers?' For you and your team to derive maximum value, no-one should know these in advance. And, for many, there is not 'one right answer'.

In fact, the final rule you should tell your team is that if someone does know the answer, don't blurt it out, as it will spoil the fun for others. On the other hand, just being silent and excluded is not a good idea – so he or she can help the group by asking them questions that will help them find the false assumption or assumptions for themselves.

Some suggestions are concealed in the text (upside down) in Chapter 7 – resist the temptation to look please until you have completed the exercise with your team.

QUESTIONING ASSUMPTIONS

1. A little girl is standing with her parents by a river, looks at their reflection in the water, and says: 'I can see all four of us'. How can this be, when there are only three people present?

2. A man goes out, sells his dog and is killed on the way home. How did he die?

3. A woman is found dead, hanging from the rafters 10 feet from the ground in a totally empty room. There is a pool of water beneath her. How did she die?

4. A man is pushing a car, which stops next to an hotel. The man immediately realises he is bankrupt. Explain.

5. How do you plant four solid cylindrical pipes so that the centre of each pipe (ie the centre of the circle) is exactly the same distance from every other pipe!

6. An archaeological team discover two, well-preserved bodies, while excavating. They positively identify the bodies as the original, biblical Adam and Eve. How can this be?

7. A naked man is found dead in the desert, clutching a straw. In his immediate vicinity, there is nothing but sand. Beyond the sand in one direction lie a number of hills. Think up an explanation that takes account of all the facts.

3

Promoting Discovery

INTRODUCTION

I hope that you found time to carry out the synergy exercise and achieve the objective: demonstrating to you and your team members how easy it is to behave as an effective team. If it did, you have already covered considerable ground towards building a better team in the workplace, and have created a momentum, from which rapid progress can be made.

In this chapter, we look at the key skills of effective questioning and listening that enable discovery by the team, make a few points on ideas and creative thinking, as well as cover the technique of 'brainstorming'. These skills and technique are ones that you should develop to become an effective team builder (ETB), and which you can develop in your team members, to enable them to become more effective.

PROMOTING DISCOVERY

It is by asking ourselves and others good questions that stretch and development is achieved, not by seeking immediate answers to remove the uncertainties that change always produces. We have seen this with the synergy exercise. The secret of effective teambuilding is to encourage the individual members to think for themselves, not simply telling them what we think is right.

To do this we need to ask the right question like: 'Just a moment, before we rush ahead, let us pause and consider what assumptions we are making in which areas?'

There are three key questions that promote discovery. You may have already discovered their nature, but in case you have not, I will provide a true story about the Alaskan Electricity Company.

The Alaskan Electricity Company faced terrible problems a few years ago. It managed over 1000 miles of overground telegraph poles, supplying electricity to a sparse and widely scattered population in very hostile weather conditions. As a result of the terrible weather, ice and snow gathered on the overhead cables, which frequently snapped under the weight. Teams of men had to travel miles and miles to repair these cables. The costs of such operations exhausted all their profits.

They solved the problem through a group of people questioning effectively. These are the questions:

Why don't we shake the poles?

But that would be difficult with over 1000 miles of poles – but, never mind, how can we develop this suggestion?

O.K. Why don't we get bears to shake the poles?

Well, yes but how can we persuade the bears to shake the poles? What will motivate the bears to shake the poles?

Well, why don't we put meat on top of the poles? In their attempts to reach the top of the poles to eat the meat, they will shake the poles and dislodge the snow and ice.

But how do we get meat to the top of the poles?

I know, why don't we use helicopters to fly the meat to the poles and place it on top for the bears?

I have a better idea. Why don't we use the helicopters to remove the ice and snow with their whirring blades and forget about the bears?

And that is what the Alaskan Electricity Company did – with considerable cost-saving resulting.

Open questions

The reason for success was the use of *open* questions as opposed to *closed* questions.

As Rudyard Kipling wrote:

I kept six honest serving men.
They taught me all I knew;
Their names were what and why and when,
And how and where and who.

The type and difference between open and closed are set out in Figure 3.1.

We all, with rare exception, have a tendency to ask closed questions.

There are three key reasons:

Our education

Our schooling is much more about finding answers – being provided with information from which we develop conclusions –

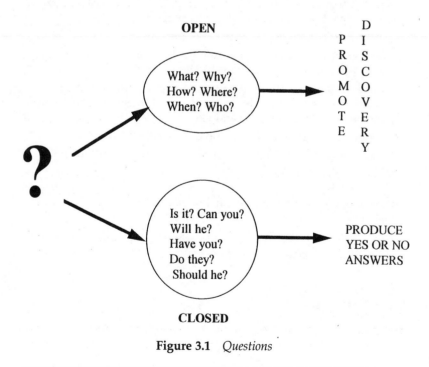

Figure 3.1 *Questions*

than it is about promoting discovery. As a result we have an inevitable bias towards questions that provide answers.

Psychology

One great advantage of closed questions is that there are immediate answers. We know subconsciously that by asking a closed question, we are guaranteeing an answer. This means that outcomes are certain and controlled. Most of us like to be in control and even if we don't, we like a degree of certainty.

With open questions, there is an unpredictability of outcomes, generating uncertainty. We could lose control of the conversation.

Ignorance

Few of us are taught about open questions.

What is more, I referred to three key questions or question types. Only three of the six open questions were used. I call these the discovery kings.

The actual sequence was:

Why, how, why, how, what, why, how, why, why?

Ask the right questions, and we will find the right answers.

When it comes to teambuilding, it is generating collective answers to critical open questions that ensures success. Some of the questions that team members need answers to are:

Why am I here and what is expected of me?

What is the purpose of the team and how will it be achieved?

What kind of leader is the 'boss' and how will he or she behave?

What will be my role and how can I carry it out well?

How will I measure up against the other team-members?

What will be the rewards for success?

Effective listening

Some managers ask their teams good and bad questions. It does not matter which, as they have no intention of listening to the answers. They have made up their minds in advance, and are going through what team members find an insulting, time-con-suming exercise in 'consultation'.

There are six reasons why listening is difficult.

Talkers are rewarded

If we go back to our upbringing, to beyond conscious memory, we learnt as babies that making a noise brought attention and satisfaction. As children, the noisiest and loudest often became the leaders and innovators of childhood games and activities. In formal education, those children who always answered questions and spoke out clearly and distinctly were more favoured and praised.

In adult and business life, the pattern continues. Those who make the most noise often gain more attention than they or their opinions deserve.

The talkers are rewarded.

We are more important

Many of us at times can consciously or subconsciously say to ourselves that we are more important than the person or people to whom we are talking. When this is the case, then we consider our views and opinions to be more important and we are unlikely to listen to anyone else's. This reality can be encouraged by status or positional power, which may be the case for you, as leader of your team.

We are the experts

A little knowledge is a dangerous thing. A lot of knowledge can be even more dangerous, when it comes to listening. It is a variation of the perception of importance theme – but this time it is not a perception that the individual or team is not important, but that what they have to say is not important. We are the experts. We say to ourselves, deep down, 'Those who know nothing have nothing to say'. Innocence and ignorance can be the source of much creativity and subsequent knowledge. Many inventions have occurred because someone did not know 'it couldn't be done', and somebody else listened!

This could be a real danger for you, once you have read this book, because you should know a little bit more about team-building than all your team members.

We think faster than we speak

This means that, as listeners, we have time available, which can either be put to good use by concentrating and trying to fully comprehend what is being said to us, or to bad use by allowing distractions and our own thoughts to intrude.

Our mind-sets

From the moment of our birth, we enter an uncertain world, with a complexity that we can never comprehend. We are therefore driven, whether consciously or not, to manage that uncertainty. Some of us are capable of tolerating, even enjoying, high levels of ambiguity and uncertainty, but for all of us there is a degree and intensity that is unbearable.

To enable us to cope, we create and confirm areas of certainty – beliefs, assumptions, attitudes and opinions that we do not consciously question. If we did, we would raise the level of uncertainty in our lives. We would be taking a risk, as we do not know what is the breaking point for us.

Our minds become set.

One consequence is that we can pre-judge, jump to hasty conclusions – hear what we want to hear, and not what is actually being said.

We can be poor speakers

The fault does not always lie with the listener. We can be poor speakers. We can speak too quickly. We can send out too much information. We can send veiled messages with unsuitable language and speech patterns or mixed messages using body language inconsistent with the words we speak.

So, with all these potential barriers to effective listening, what do we need to do to ensure we do not waste our good questions, because we do not really hear the answers?

The keys to effective listening are:

❑ Concentration and focus on the speaker – emptying our heads of our own thoughts and concerns.
❑ The right body language. For instance, by sitting still – neither fidgeting nor pencil-tapping, with an open posture (arms not folded or behind the head, and the back straight or leaning slightly forward), warm eye contact (no eye-balling or staring out of the window) and the occasional nod or helpful murmur.
❑ Feedback to confirm understanding: 'So let me see. You think that we should . . .'
❑ No premature judgement.

CREATIVE THINKING

What is an idea?

This may seem to be a strange question, but bear with me. In fact, take a pencil and paper and jot down an area where there could be improvement, eg increasing sales in your organisation or any area you like. Then, having identified the area, write down a few ideas that will cause improvement.

If we take the example of sales, and consider the question how we could increase sales, we could:

❑ Hire more salespeople.
❑ Cut price of products or services.
❑ Spend more on training.
❑ Improve morale of salesforce.

Now let us look at these ideas. They are simply actions or action areas. Hiring more salespeople is an action, cutting the price of products or services is an action, spending more on training is an action and improving morale is an area where actions are required if morale is to be improved and sales increased.

So, ideas are simply actions that need to be taken or action areas where more ideas or alternative actions need to be developed.

Two interesting implications follow:

1. Experts try to separate out logical and creative thinking and give creative thinking a mystique and a degree of difficulty that can, quite understandably, put off logical, pragmatic types. Think of the words 'brainstorming', 'conceptualisation', 'blue sky thinking'! How much more valuable and relevant is it to say to a group – your team: 'Let us get together to think up alternative actions we need to take to solve the particular problem or issue we face!'

2. The more logical we are, the more creative we can be. I have always been taken by Edward de Bono's model of creative thinking. He postulates that the brain operates in stable thought patterns, and we tend to move logically from one stable state to a connected one. To have a good idea we need to provoke the brain from its comfortable path, suspend judgement and generate movement. Then, in a flash, the good idea comes to us – but is only recognised if we connect back logically to where we started. So, we cannot generate ideas by logical foresight, but will only recognise a good idea in logical hindsight. There is a complete analogy with humour. We do not understand the comedian until the punchline – the illogicality – and only laugh if we can connect back logically. If we do not, we say: 'I don't understand that'.

So, the more humour we generate, the more ideas we will have, and the more logical we are, the more ideas we will have – provided we suspend judgement. That's the difficult bit, because the more logical we are, the greater has our critical faculty been developed!

You may well have found that this is what happened in your synergy exercise – already proving the points made. I certainly know of a Fellow of the Chartered Accountants, who was prepared to get involved in group action thinking (or brainstorming as it is more commonly known), played by the rules and discovered just how creative he was – much to his delight, as he had, up until then, seen himself as very uncreative and diminished as a result.

Group action thinking (GAT) or brainstorming

This is an incredibly powerful tool, which is at the core of building an effective team and becoming a better teambuilder. However, as is always the case, to achieve optimum effect, there needs to be structure, process and one golden rule.

As regards process, which will be developed in more detail in Chapter 6, you must remember that brainstorming, or action thinking, always occurs separately from evaluation, at the appropriate time and phase of an agreed process. So you might use it to uncover false assumptions, or to explore the alternative actions or options available to solve a particular problem – indeed whenever there is time for opening up, rather than closing down. In short, whenever you pose the team an open question, particularly one of the discovery kings – why, what and how.

In a discovery phase, there should be a time limit for alternative actions to be generated and you, as ETB, need to explain and enforce the golden rule that *no-one is allowed to criticise by word or body language.*

This rule has been mentioned implicitly before, and is covered explicitly now. Criticism kills ideas. In extreme situations, where a so-called teambuilder has and abuses positional power over team members, his or her criticism of the first idea will stop the flow of ideas, leaving only one to be adopted – and you can guess the originator of that idea!

If the logic of criticism had been applied to the Alaskan situation at any time, the ultimate solution could never have been found. For instance: 'Don't be ridiculous, there are over a 1000 miles of poles, far too many to be shaken!' or 'It just won't work.' 'Research indicates that there are only 100 bears, far too few to shake the poles. In any case, with respect, the suggestion that bears would shake telegraph poles is far too fanciful', and so on.

Body language must not be ignored – the accidental or deliberate hostile response by look or body movement can do the trick just as well as words. The rule needs to be understood and agreed by all beforehand and then monitored by the facilitator, whether you, the ETB, or someone else appointed to the role.

So 'silly' ideas must be tolerated, and not killed off under the withering fire of criticism, as they can lead to new insights and useful perspectives. Silliness for its own sake is not a good idea – but the De Bono techniques of reversal – reversing the logic of an idea, or exaggerating it, can be very useful.

For instance, one group, looking at how to be more creative came up with 'spend more time on creative thinking' and someone reversed it: 'spend less time!' Subsequent consideration of that led to the recognition that some problems are best ignored as they go away (as they were not important after all) or get solved by someone else. Additionally, it is often wise not to wrestle with the problem at night, but focus on getting to sleep, as you wake up refreshed and having solved the problem in your sleep – the land of illogic and provocation!

Generating atmosphere with a few dry runs on some humorous issues is recommended, which is why I suggested the synergy exercise, as your team will now be warm to effective brainstorming. There can be an enormous difference in output between a group which is cold and hesitant and one that is relaxed and smiling.

A flipchart or whiteboard will be necessary, so that there is a visual display of ideas, or the group can stick post-it notes around the walls. In the former case, there will need to be a scribe or facilitator, who is also a contributor. In the latter case, the ideas should be verbally articulated as well as written down. In both cases, someone needs to ensure that the no criticism rule is followed.

Benefits

The creative output will be far higher than that of any individual, as the synergy exercise should have demonstrated. We all have our mind-sets, our limited background, experience and knowledge. By opening our minds, sharing our ideas and allowing those sparks to be generated, we all become more creative and the whole always exceeds the sum of the individual parts.

This also holds for evaluation. We can only tap into ourselves.

The combined wealth of knowledge and experience of the group makes evaluation quicker and more effective.

Fundamental improvements in work processes will occur. GAT can be applied to issue identification, problem solving, project definition, writing a scoping paper, planning and so on. It can be used for group tasks *and* individual tasks at any vital stage. Increasingly, it becomes informal and swift. Other team members are happy to be involved for four reasons:

1. It improves the efficiency and effectiveness of a colleague's output.
2. As it is reciprocated, it improves the efficiency and effectiveness of their own work.
3. The knowledge of the group about each individual's key work activities expands enormously. This makes it much easier to take up the reins when a colleague is sick or on leave.
4. Team morale soars.

It is the way to generate a shared vision, common understanding, agreed objectives and a sense of unity and direction – it is the pivotal team-building tool.

Finally, there are a few pitfalls to avoid.

Number of ideas

There can be a temptation to go for quantity rather than quality. One writer and practitioner proudly told his readers that he had achieved, through one GAT, over 100 restatements of the problem, and over 1000 ideas! Evaluation took months.

Quality is much more important. Often, you will get 20 or so alternative actions, half of which can be integrated into a structured action plan – great!

The no criticism rule must take primacy, but it is worth creating an environment where there is no pressure for contribution and where silence is recognised as a creative act.

Numbers

Many experts recommend up to 20, acknowledging that some individuals will not contribute – presumably sacrificing atmosphere and the individual on the altar of quantity. GAT is best as a team or small group process, with numbers not exceeding eight or less than four.

Event

GAT can be seen as a major and rare event, reserved for a major strategic issue, attended by a select group, usually off-site and expensive. There is a place for that, especially where the top team is involved. But it can give the wrong cultural messages – particularly that GAT is not a cheap, effective, work-based, regular group activity.

Isolation

GAT is sometimes carried out in isolation. Evaluation is done later, occasionally by different people. GAT should be an integral part of problem solving and action planning, carried out by the same people, often in the same session, as it is part of a clearly defined process.

4

HOW GROUPS BEHAVE

INTRODUCTION

In this chapter, we look at how groups behave: in particular what stages or phases a group passes through, from being immature to becoming a performing or effective team.

For us to have a complete understanding, it is important that we have considered first the stages or levels of development of the individual.

Finally, we look at a complete model dealing with the interactions of the individual, the group and the task and consider what the ETB needs to do to build an effective team.

LEVELS OF INDIVIDUAL DEVELOPMENT

Figure 4.1 sets out the stages or levels of individual development.

Within a day, an individual can move one level up or down. Over time an individual can move one level up or down. An understanding of the nature of each level and behaviours demonstrated, as well as the causes of movement, will benefit the ETB enormously, when building his or her team, as well the translation from the individual to the group context, covered in the next section.

Figure 4.1 includes only three levels, as I do not intend to cover the base level: fighting for *survival*. Sadly, there are some areas of the world where much of the populace operates at this level, as well as many individuals in developed countries – such as the

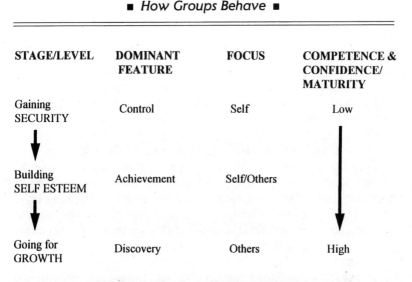

STAGE/LEVEL	DOMINANT FEATURE	FOCUS	COMPETENCE & CONFIDENCE/ MATURITY
Gaining SECURITY	Control	Self	Low
Building SELF ESTEEM	Achievement	Self/Others	
Going for GROWTH	Discovery	Others	High

Figure 4.1 *Levels of individual development*

homeless and many of the unemployed. But for those in work, the base level does not apply.

Security

However, gaining security does apply. We are considering the individual at this juncture, and there are three main situations where we can be operating at the security level.

Unfamiliar situation

In an unfamiliar situation, like a new job where we feel uncertain about things, we may lack confidence in our abilities, and feel a measure of fear in facing the unknown. We may put a brave face on things, display confidence, or even over-confidence, to the outside world – our new employers or our new leader and team-members – but the reality for most, if not all, will be a feeling of insecurity and the need to develop some certainty in the situation.

The key word used is 'control' – in that we will want to gain some control over this unfamiliar environment and future. Just as importantly, we will be open or vulnerable to control.

A strong visionary leader can quite easily take charge of immature followers, and provide the sense of purpose and direction they need. In fact, some companies' cultures are based on this reality. Equally, for many citizens in countries which have been hit hard by the recession – producing uncertainty and reducing the development level of the nation as a whole – the cry has gone up: 'Give us the strong visionary leader we need.'

As leaders, whether of individuals or teams, we have to recognise this reality for others and help the follower or team member gain a feeling of security so that ascent to the next level of development can be achieved. Clearly part of the process is to provide answers to all the unanswered questions – the specifics are addressed in Chapter 6.

As the result of an unexpected change, perceived negatively

We will cover this in detail in Chapter 7. How confident we were before the event, and how significant the event was, will determine whether the impact simply reduces our self-esteem or threatens our need for security.

A natural state

A few people, for whatever reasons – often to do with upbringing – can spend much of their adult life at this level of development. It could be argued that the leader, who displays an excess of control in his or her leadership approach, is doing so in response to inner feelings of insecurity and lack of confidence. The overt manifestation is over-confidence, control of others, and the imposition of such unspoken rules like the 'I am infallible' rule.

With a total and necessary focus on self, such leaders have massive egos and need constant reassurance as to their competence and effectiveness. They also take any form of criticism or challenge extremely badly, as that threatens their insecure base of being.

It goes without saying that such leaders are incapable of building an effective team, as they deny permanently the necessary learning for themselves and their team members.

Having said that, if a leader like that genuinely wants to build a team, he or she would have to enjoy experientially based learning, resulting in their becoming part of an effective team.

Self-esteem

Most of us spend most of the time at this level – building our self-esteem – developing competence and confidence. What constitutes success will depend on what we value. The common denominator is achievement: whether in material terms, making money and 'bettering ourselves'; in career terms, climbing the career ladder to perceived success; in relationship terms, being an effective partner and/or parent; or achieving specific personal goals – running marathons, writing books, winning at a host of sports and so on.

Clearly, for some, success is measured by a combination, and for others there is focus on but one area. It is probably true that lasting success will only come from a balanced and holistic approach. I have seen many men, who have focused on career to the exclusion of relationships or personal development, come complete croppers when forced to retire. Many women, locked too long into caring roles, find fulfilment in later years very difficult.

Again, this is why the team – the true team – is such an incredibly powerful development tool for the individual. The balance is part of an effective team, and has to be created by the teambuilder, so the team can become effective.

When effective, difficult tasks or projects are successfully completed, personal relationships successfully managed and each individual is learning and growing.

When a team is effective, all the individuals are operating at the highest level – the growth level.

Growth level

At this level, we believe in ourselves, we value ourselves, we have high self-esteem and are competent and confident in our abilities. Because of this, we can focus externally on others, and try to answer questions that are too difficult to face when at a lower level.

We can give without having to receive, we can learn without having to lead, we can listen without having to talk. We can coach an individual or build an effective team.

The key word is discovery. Because we have the confidence to question and explore, take risks and learn, we discover – new insights and perspectives, new challenges to face, and new solutions to old problems. And the heart of the discovery process is dialogue, whether on an individual or team basis.

It is the ability of an effective team to discover, through the highly developed questioning and listening skills of each team member, which produces synergy and offers the most powerful way of managing change. This is because the heart of successful change management, given that change is defined as 'making or becoming different', is discovery.

IMPACT ON BEHAVIOUR

The development level at which we are operating will have a major impact on our behaviour.

At the security level, we are very much focused on ourselves and our needs. This will make us poor leaders and it will be impossible to build an effective team. We will use a 'command and control' leadership style, treating followers as 'robots' to carry out our wishes – setting rather than agreeing objectives, telling and checking, criticising and blaming, and relying on our positional power and the use of the stick and the carrot to get our own way.

We are simply too busy focusing on ourselves to have any effective regard for other people. As a result, we do not realise the impact our behaviour has on our followers. I know many followers who receive this leadership approach some or even most of the time from their bosses. What often is not appreciated by these followers is that it is usually thoughtlessness on such bosses' parts. Bosses, operating at the security level, only have time to think about themselves. It is not deliberate, Machiavellian, or because the follower is disliked. Too many followers take impersonal treatment personally.

The effective follower tries to help his or her boss develop, not sulk in silence or undermine the boss or, eventually 'kick against the pricks' and find his career stalled or terminated.

I have been assuming that leaders operating at the security level have a task focus, which is normally the case. Their behaviours can broadly be described as aggressive, insisting on their rights without any regard for their responsibilities.

Incidentally, delegation is completely ineffective as it is dumping, disappearing and then interfering.

Occasionally, there are leaders operating at security level who are relationship focused. In such cases, the behaviours are non-assertive and manipulative.

When developing our self-esteem, there will be a difference in our behaviour, depending on whether our main driver is achieving tasks, achieving quality relationships, or both. If both, we will start to listen to our followers and be able to provide more and more effective support, while retaining a measure of control. Delegation becomes more effective, though it is not coaching – promoting discovery – simply enabling the follower to become more effective in doing things our way. It is more effective 'push' or teaching, not coaching.

If the focus is tasks or relationships, there is not much change. There is an interesting reality with 'carers', which I only noticed recently. When we are building our self-esteem, we are necessarily driven by our value systems. If we care for others, we try to help them, but not effectively from the other person's point of view, because we are operating still from our values, which we try to impart.

I overheard a mother talking to a son, which brought home this message.

☞ **EXAMPLE** ☜

Mother: 'What would you like for your supper. I could do you cheeseburger and chips, or soup and baked beans on toast.'

Son: 'I'll have cheeseburger and chips.'

Mother: 'That's not very healthy: you should have soup, baked beans on toast, and a piece of fruit to finish. That's much better for you.'

Son: 'But I want cheeseburger and chips. You said I could have that.'

Mother: 'But, Paul, it's not a very healthy meal. Come on now, have the soup and baked beans on toast, and an apple just to please your mother, eh?'

Son: 'OK, mum.'

What is also noticeable, when leaders are developing their self-esteem, is that individualism reigns supreme. We do not build effective teams, whatever the structures and however often we have team meetings.

We have individual relationships with followers, and have a spectrum of attitudes from the favourite to the 'trouble-maker'.

We personalise the behaviours demonstrated by our followers. We do not value difference!

STAGES OF TEAM DEVELOPMENT

In this section, we look at the stages or phases that teams go through from the moment of formation to the moment of effective performance. The stages are linked to development levels, because a team can be considered as an individual entity that passes from immaturity to maturity through the careful and effective deployment of knowledge and skill by you, the ETB.

Figure 4.2 sets out the stages, differentiating between the four – confusion, conflict, co-operation and commitment – which are

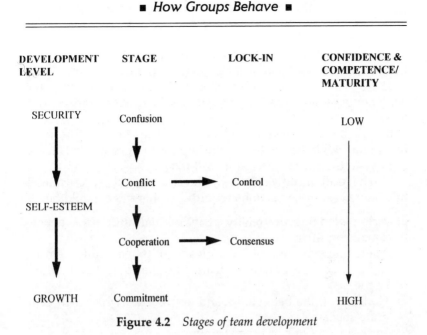

Figure 4.2 *Stages of team development*

part of a progression and from which the group can easily move, and the two – control and consensus – which can become stable states for considerable periods of time. We deal with each in turn.

Confusion

When a group forms ie meets for the first time, the group will be at a low level of development – it will be immature. The individuals will be in a new, unfamiliar situation, and there will be a high degree of confusion due to the unfamiliarity and uncertainty generated by a new environment.

They will be concerned with themselves rather than others and in meeting their security needs. They tend to be closed – cautious, reserved and wary. Some may think positively about this new team, but will be impatient with the muddle and confusion – wanting structure and purpose, and annoyed at its absence. Others will want to be somewhere else, anywhere else, and will feel exposed and awkward. They will perceive the rest of their team members, and particularly the leader, who has caused this unpleasant situation, as hostile.

There will tend to be little communication, lots of silences and unpleasant pauses. People will be polite – on their best behaviour.

There will be a dependency on you, and a need for your leadership, because the team members will be at or near security level.

It will be your behaviours and your actions at this first, inevitably transitory stage of developing the group, that holds the key to the course the group will take.

You have all the power. We will develop the full process model in Chapter 6, but key actions required at this stage would be:

❑ Acknowledging the reality of individual attitudes – depersonalising them.
❑ Managing expectations – your leadership/teambuilding role, the desired direction of the team, and the context and nature of the task.
❑ Confirming the behaviours and approaches which will generate success.
❑ Introducing GAT or brainstorming.

Conflict

We have already discovered the list of behaviours and actions that can take place in this phase, which can predominate for poorly led groups, and to which performing teams can revert under the impact of changes, perceived negatively (see Chapter 7).

Typical behaviours are:

❑ Individuals creating their own power-base – confrontation, rebellion and sub-grouping.
❑ Feeling isolated and excluded – opting out.
❑ Not confident in role allocated.
❑ No sense of direction or purpose.
❑ Hidden agendas, and behind-the-scenes manoeuvres.
❑ Individuals deliberately undermining the authority of the leader.
❑ Poor time-keeping.
❑ Having cold water poured on your ideas.

The key question is how do you, the ETB, ensure this phase is transitory or even non-existent?

There is a terrible mistake that many companies and teambuilders make in their efforts to build teams – the separation of task and relationship achievement. What happens is that the teambuilder goes on a teambuilding event – perhaps in an outdoor environment, but certainly 'off-site'. Often, within a few days, the bonding has occurred. Then the team returns to its normal working environment, and, within a very short period of time, the conflict phase rears its ugly head again – much to the teambuilder's surprise and therefore annoyance.

It is by the power of process and the application of team techniques like brainstorming which help the ETB create the right environment. It is through the acknowledgement of uncertainty and the management of expectations; it is through a shared visioning process involving each individual in this positive environment; it is the agreement of objectives, roles and so on which creates the bonding essential to team performance.

A good ETB does not need outside help. He or she manages a seamless and swift passage to performance or the 'commitment' level. As developed in Chapter 6, the key to success is timing – what should and can be achieved at each meeting. As you will have already demonstrated with the synergy exercise, much more can be achieved than we think possible.

There is a danger, which a whole book on teambuilding can accentuate or even trigger, that teambuilders believe that the whole business of teambuilding is so fraught with difficulty that only a little can be achieved in a long time.

Knowledge, competence and self-belief, like faith, can move mountains.

Control

As mentioned earlier in this chapter, a strong, dominant leader with a clear vision can effectively sell it to a group of individuals who are operating at a low level of development, as their needs for security will be satisfied.

The group becomes an imperfect instrument to carry out the leader's wishes. Because security needs include emotional needs, the bonding mechanism is the leader himself or herself. In the extreme, there is a cult of personality and clones of varying competence.

There is no synergy as there is no discovery.

There is no development for the follower, as there is no learning.

The society – it is not a team – becomes very closed and introverted, to avoid external stimuli that might interfere with or jeopardise the leader's control.

Such groups or societies can be successful for sustained periods, because of the focus and commitment of the followers. They inevitably die when the leader dies or, in business terms, retires or is replaced.

If the leader is dominant but not a visionary, then control will be partial and spasmodic, and most of the time will be spent in the conflict phase.

Co-operation

Under an ETB, there is a swift transition to the co-operative stage – the stepping stone to the final mature stage of the 'commitment level'. Individuals respond to the positive environment that the ETB is creating, they respond to a leader, who behaves exactly as he or she wants them to behave, and they respond to techniques like brainstorming, where they are visibly involved in the decision-making process.

As a result the mind-sets and attitudes operating at the 'confusion' level undergo a sea change.

A sense of identity with the group emerges, and group members are prepared to change preconceived ideas or opinions on the basis of facts presented by other group members.

Questioning and listening skills improve. If conflict arises, it is dealt with as a mutual problem for the group and not individually based with winners and losers.

At this stage, feedback helps the bonding and the performance.

Consensus

There can be a distortion or cul-de-sac, called the lock-in stage of 'consensus'.

It is particularly prevalent with groups of peers like partners in a partnership, which often operate as self-managing groups. It also holds for informal events with social overtones like 'strategy events' or 'away-days'.

The focus of the group is the relationships, where everyone feels very comfortable with each other and the team. What emerges is called 'group think' or 'one for all': the individualistic element, the challenge, the drive for discovery, is lost.

Individuals are reluctant to disturb the harmony by injecting controversy. If and when an idea or solution emerges, then everyone enthusiastically supports it. Getting things done can take forever – as the group flows in one direction and then another – all together, but not focused on or committed to task achievement.

One major drawback to the consensus stage, if it occurs, is that it is difficult to progress to effective teamwork, because all the group members think they are already there!

Commitment

We know what a team operating at the 'commitment' level looks and feels like, and you, as ETB, will have already experienced it. It is not a steady-state situation but a dynamic one, as the sharing of ideas, energy, understanding and commitment will lead the team to different directions than were initially envisaged, and to levels of performance that could not have been anticipated at the outset.

A major issue for the ETB will be to ensure that the challenges and horizons can be expanded, so that the team can continually grow and perform.

INTERACTION OF INDIVIDUALS, GROUP AND TASK

Task requirements

We are in business to achieve results. Any task or project we undertake, whether individually or collectively in a group, has its own dimensions and complexity. There are certain requirements in terms of people, process and resources that need to be understood and managed if the desired result is going to be achieved.

Individual needs

Individuals have certain needs, particular dispositions and orientations. The extent to which individuals completing tasks can be motivated, and feel that their needs are recognised and fulfilled, will have a major impact on the quality of task outcomes. Individuals, although unique, can demonstrate a narrow range of similar behaviours, depending on what development level they are operating from. Individuals have potential to grow and to operate at a higher level of performance than they themselves think possible.

Group dynamics

The group itself can be seen to have a life of its own, to be an entity in its own right. Pressures from the dynamics of the group can affect, if not determine, the behaviour of individuals. In the context of work teams, we have seen six possible manifestations of group dynamics – the six Cs – confusion, conflict, control, co-operation, consensus and commitment.

In most groups, there tends to be too great a focus on the task, and not enough on individual needs. Additionally, there is one individual who has the ability to try to satisfy his or her perceived needs – the leader, with positional power. The satisfaction of those needs is often to the detriment of the needs of the rest of the team, forced to operate in a subordinate position.

The outcome tends to be 'negergy', see Figure 4.3. This initial model was developed by John Adair.

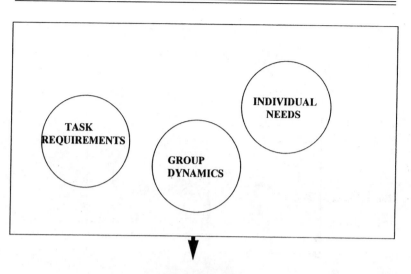

"NEGERGY"

Figure 4.3 *Impact of traditional leader*

IMPACT OF ETB

However, you are not a conventional leader – you are aiming to become an effective teambuilder, which is infinitely more rewarding than managing groups that produce 'negergy' without ever knowing why.

Figure 4.4. indicates the role of the ETB in producing an effective team. The goal for the ETB is to produce an alignment of the needs of the individual, the dynamics of the group and the requirements of the task with the result that a high-performing, 'synergy' team is produced.

The keys to unlock this outcome are vision, mission and process. Figure 4.5 develops and connects these through applying a simple powerful model, based on work by Ned Herrmann.

The left side focuses on task, using logic, analysis, systems and processes to define and implement the task. The right side focuses on people, using creativity, intuition and emotion to

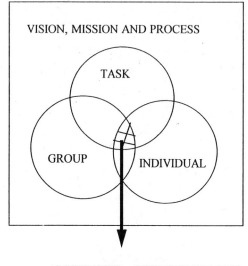

VISION, MISSION AND PROCESS

ALIGNMENT = HIGH-PERFORMING
SYNERGY TEAM

Figure 4.4 *Impact of ETB*

define the vision and implement the vision through achieving the values supporting it.

The effective leader of the future is the co-ordinator of process and not controller of people – applying process to develop a shared understanding of the *team vision* and *task mission*, and then helping the team develop and apply the processes required to formulate and implement the strategy to turn the vision into reality and the mission into a triumph of achievement.

For the approach to be integrated, there must be interlinking between the task and the people, the mission and the vision , and how this is achieved is covered in Chapter 6.

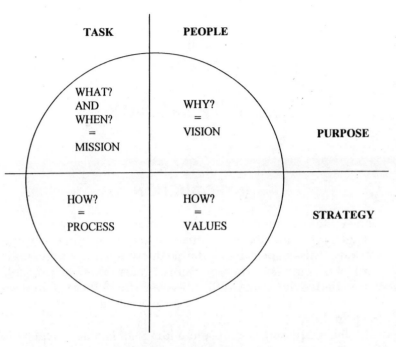

Figure 4.5 *Integrated approach*

THE TEAM MIX

INTRODUCTION

One key to becoming a better teambuilder is to recognise what strengths you and the individuals in the team bring to teamworking. This chapter uses a simple questionnaire, based on the work of the eminent expert on teams, Professor Belbin, to enable you to derive the team profile, discover where there is duplication or omission of strength and develop strategies to optimise the team mix.

In the early stages of teambuilding, it is vital to play to strengths, as that will develop the competence and confidence of team members. As the power of the team is unleashed, and each individual appreciates the strengths of fellow team members, then positive feedback rather than negative criticism will enable each individual to develop new strengths and compensating strategies for any weaknesses that diminish team performance.

The *team strengths audit* (TSA) is printed at the end of this section, enabling it to be photocopied so that each team member can complete it.

I would suggest that only you complete it at this stage, and leave the completion by your colleagues until you have developed your action plan, set out in the final chapter of the book. My view is that the completion of the audit should be part of the teambuilding process, agreed by your team and completed at a time when all members are present. Information is power and if you ask for individuals to complete and return it to you on an individual basis, in their perception you will be behaving in a way that is inconsistent with the open behaviour you will need to demonstrate, if you are to be a better teambuilder or ETB.

After the section covering the TSA, we look at the practical use, considering the complete set of strengths or competences and then focusing on omissions and duplications.

TEAM STRENGTHS AUDIT

Your Preferences

Please read the eight strength classifications in the table on the next two pages, and the description of activities and actions, related to each strength. Then consider, when you are working in a team, how you prefer contributing. When you have studied each category, decide your order of preference, from 1 to 8, enter that in the column marked Preference and then allocate the points, according to the table below, in the column marked Points.

Preference	Points
1st	21
2nd	14
3rd	9
4th	6
5th	4
6th	3
7th	2
8th	1
Total	60

Strength	Activities/Actions	Preference	Points
INVESTIGATING	☐ Looking for the latest ideas and developments ☐ Developing and using contacts outside the team ☐ Taking advantage of new opportunities ☐ Opening up discussions to stimulate thinking		
INNOVATING	☐ Developing new insights and perspectives on problems ☐ Making original contributions ☐ Finding areas to stretch the imagination ☐ Producing ideas		
EVALUATING	☐ Analysing situations and weighing up possible choices ☐ Providing an objective outlook and cool judgement ☐ Putting a case for alternative actions ☐ Finding a line of argument to refute unsound propositions		
FOCUSING	☐ Focusing the group on the task at hand ☐ Exercising strong influence on decisions and pushing for action ☐ Willing to take the lead in the absence of progress ☐ Prepared to challenge the views of others		

Strength	Activities/Actions	Preference	Points
IMPLEMENTING	☐ Finding practical solutions to problems ☐ Turning plans to reality ☐ Organising essential work ☐ Operating well in a structured framework		
FINISHING	☐ Paying attention to detail ☐ Preventing careless mistakes and omissions being made ☐ Giving tasks complete attention ☐ Pushing to get tasks completed on time		
SUPPORTING	☐ Working well with different people ☐ Promoting a good team atmosphere ☐ Supporting good suggestions in the common interest ☐ Interested in developing good relationships with team members		
CO-ORDINATING	☐ Drawing out team-members' views and opinions ☐ Influencing without exerting pressure ☐ Developing agreement in the team ☐ Co-ordinating the activities of team members		

PRACTICAL USE

This section enables you to have prior strategic thought before the general results are shared and known – to recognise where pitfalls may lie. However, assuming the TSA is carried out on a team basis, the team itself will be in a position, as facilitated by you, to determine the strategies required to avoid 'personality clashes' or cater for the omission of a required strength.

A final caveat. You and your team members have indicated preferences and not ability. We can have a low preference for a particular strength, and still be competent, though probably stressed. Equally, we can have a strong preference for a particular approach, and not necessarily be very good at it, although we are likely to think we are! However, the more we like to do something, the more we will do it, and the better we will become. Practice does not make perfect, but tends to improve competence.

One of the great advantages of the explicit sharing of preference and the fitting of strength into a clearly defined process is that it increases its effective use.

We consider first the complete set of strengths and how they produce optimum performance. As a workable approach, a 'strength' can be defined as a first or second preference, with the third or fourth choices as back-ups, which can be developed by an individual, if it is required for effective team performance. It is less stressful and more effective if we develop competence in areas we like operating in rather than the reverse.

Complete set

Please refer to Figure 5.1.

The first point to make is that all the strengths are required for optimal team performance. Creativity (combining investigating and innovating) is vital for effective discovery, Analysis (combining evaluating and finishing) is vital to achieve a practical, workable approach, Drive (combining implementing and focusing) is vital to ensuring the project actually gets completed and Harmony (combining co-ordinating and supporting) is vital to

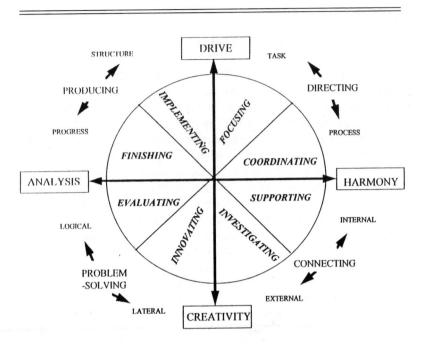

Figure 5.1 *Team strength circle*

ensure the group becomes an effective team. (As an aside, this circle links to the 'integrated' approach set out at the end of Chapter 4, with analysis and drive on the 'left' side of the brain and 'creativity' and 'harmony' on the 'right' side.)

At the next level, we can see how each strength contributes to Problem-solving, Producing, Directing and Connecting. For example, co-ordinating can be seen as directing process which helps in the creation of harmony, and focusing can be seen as directing task, helping to create the drive for results.

If one strength is missing, then the team goes out of balance, and its performance will suffer. For instance, without investigating, the team will become too introverted and will be seen as a culturally deviant unit, as no connections are being made to the outside world in the shape of sponsors, other teams, departments and so on. If there is no process or process co-ordinating, the chances are that there will never be any synergy, as the team will be highjacked by whoever is strongest in focusing, who will be pushing too hard on the task side, upset other team members' sensitivities and leave the team in a permanent state of conflict or control, or a combination.

The second point to make is that there are potential tensions in the system, specifically between individuals with different strengths or strength combinations that fall exclusively in the 'left' set as compared to the 'right' set. For instance, someone strong in focusing and implementing – very much a task orientation – will view someone with co-ordinating and supporting – very much a people orientation – as indecisive, lacking drive and wishy-washy. The reverse perspective would be someone who is too pushy, ego-focused, insensitive and a poor listener.

Equally the evaluating, finishing combination might be viewed as too critical, individualistic and nit-picking, and so on.

One of the advantages of an explicit identification of strength preference is that these perceptions can be brought into the open, and the value and need for different strengths recognised and appreciated. Potential clashes can be de-personalised and dealt with through developing a process, which requires the use of the different strengths as an agreed and integral part of developing and achieving the team vision and task mission.

Omissions

A team will be able to maximise performance if, when operating together as a team, it has the complete range of strengths available to be deployed. If there is an absence, then it needs to be identified and the skill or strength developed.

For instance, one of the least prevalent strengths among individuals is the finishing strength – partly because managers have so many balls in the air, they can rarely, on an individual and personal basis, see the task through to conclusion. It has to be delegated in part or completely. This also explains why projects are so rarely completed on time and in budget.

It is a very necessary team skill, as are all the others. Part of the problem, assuming there is one, is resolved by having an effective team process, covered in Chapter 6, but it is also necessary to allocate that role to a team member, who has some existing skill. It may be yourself, it may not.

The great advantage of this clearly allocated and agreed role is not only that the project will get finished – but it gives permission for a specific individual to check progress, check the detail and push for the meeting of agreed deadlines. Such an explicit approach eliminates or greatly reduces the probability of 'personality clashes'.

If an individual has this strength in abundance, but there is no permission as there is no effective team process, he or she is likely to deploy this strength, but understandably may well be perceived as an 'interfering so-and-so'. If you carry out the role implicitly as a leader, then hey presto, there is a perception gap.

The same holds for all the roles. If someone is strong in supporting, and it is not you the ETB, you can use that strength to help the bonding required for an effective team. Incidentally, if the process is right, then everyone will develop at least two strengths that may not be there to start with – innovating and supporting.

As said before, perhaps on more than one occasion (!), the team is a very powerful and positive learning device for the individual.

In fact, it could be argued that, if a team operates for sustained periods of time at the commitment level, every individual develops all the team strengths. The probability is increased by developing and applying a process, where there is disaggregation into a defined order of the activities required to build a team and complete a task effectively.

Duplications

Duplication of strengths can also lead to 'personality clashes' as well as differences. Most of the duplications, if recognised, become an advantage fairly easily, if any tasks allocated during the process recognise the duplication.

So, if you have two or more team-members supporting in the development process, that is great. You have much more of a problem if every team-member has a low preference in supporting! Provided innovating is a specific part of the process, one of the activities separated out, then having two or more creative thinkers is fine. Similarly, if evaluation is a defined separate task for the team, then having more than one evaluating is good news.

With two or more strong in investigating, that can be allocated to a subgroup of those with good networks or allocated to one individual, with the others 'suppressed' with their agreement. This is a matter of judgement, and time. If time only permits individual investigation, then allocate it to the team member, whose only strength it is, if that is the case, or to the individual, who has other strengths duplicated by other team members.

With duplication of implementing, if task completion requires subgroups, each of which requiring a task implementer, there is no problem – otherwise only one should manage the implementation phase of the team project. Finishing also comes into its own, when the agreed strategy is being implemented individually or in subgroups. If subgroups are involved, then each will value the finishing skill. If it is only individuals implementing agreed action plans, then there is only room for one applying the finishing skill.

The two problem-children are focusing and co-ordinating, as focusing defines aspects of the traditional leadership role, and co-ordinating is a necessary and critical skill for you, as the ETB. We will deal with each in turn.

Focusing

On a leadership and team-development programme, there were 22 senior managers, including a board member, of a diversified manufacturing company. Early on they undertook, in groups of five or six, an exercise that measured team synergy. Three of the four groups produced various degrees of synergy, after every individual had agreed the behaviours and processes required to be effective.

One group of six produced 'negergy' with some amusement and comment from the other group, and embarrassment to themselves.

The next exercise was to discover team strengths. Four out of the six members of the group with 'negergy' were strong in focusing. They were all keen to 'focus the group on the task at hand, exercise strong influence on decisions, push for action, take the lead in the absence of progress, and challenge the view of others'. There was an awful lot of heat and very little light. You will know in what stage of team development they spent the exercise!

All strengths are necessary to team performance. Taking the case, where you and you only are strong in focusing, then simply discipline yourself to apply that strength when it is appropriate in the process, using the co-ordinating strength you will need to have or develop at other times – you will make an excellent ETB.

Taking the case when you and one other are strong in focusing, then this is an issue – a potential challenge to your leadership position – which needs to be specifically addressed. It will be necessary for one of you to reduce the use, and play to or develop another strength.

The probability of implicit or explicit clashes increases, the more team members exhibit this strength. With three or more, there may be the need to change team membership or recognise that achieving synergy will take a long time and a lot of conscious effort by all parties.

As an aside, if you have control over selection of your team or of any replacement, you can use the TSA to hire an individual who provides a missing strength or avoids creating a problem in duplication, that is going to create difficulties in the future. It is interesting that, as mentioned in Tom Peters' video *The Leadership Alliance*, one US company – Johnsonville Sausage Makers – re-organised, very profitably, on a work-team basis, and the work teams took on the whole range of traditional management responsibilities, including the hiring and firing of team members. You can see why.

Co-ordinating

This is your role as ETB, and a strength you need to develop if absent. In the teambuilding stage, if one team member has this strength, you could delegate without 'losing face'. For instance, he or she would make a good facilitator, whenever discovery is being promoted.

Otherwise, he or she can play to or develop other strengths. One positive aspect to the duplication of this strength is that, if you have to be absent, you know who would make a good deputy, and be accepted by the team, given that what is required is process control rather than 'command and control'.

Well, this completes the audit chapter. Understanding your team mix and agreeing strategies to ensure the deployment of the whole range of strengths, the effective use of existing strengths and the eradication of potential 'personality' clashes is a key part of becoming a better teambuilder.

6

THE POWER OF PROCESS

INTRODUCTION

This is a very pragmatic chapter and covers specific processes to achieve specific objectives.

A process is a series of actions or activities carried out in a specified order that, if effectively co-ordinated, will maximise the probability of achieving the desired outcome in both an efficient and effective manner.

As highlighted in earlier chapters, the ETB's leadership role is not to control the team-members but to promote discovery of the right processes and to co-ordinate the effective implementation of those agreed processes.

We look at specific processes to achieve the following objectives:

1. Promote discovery
2. Create a team vision
3. Complete a team task
4. Run a successful meeting
5. Build a team.

We are not suggesting that you slavishly follow these processes, nor impose them on your team, as that would be completely counter-productive. They are provided because they have been implemented successfully by managers in the workplace, and provide you with necessary knowledge to enable you to help the team be successful in what it does. Your team members will need some guidance from you to start with, particularly with 'promoting discovery' – to get the ball rolling as it were – as they know much less than you about how to build a successful team.

When a group is at the 'confusion' level, we know there needs to be some direction and guidance to remove the feelings of insecurity and uncertainty that are present. The difference between you, as ETB, and a conventional leader is that the conventional leader tends to give immediate guidance on how to complete the task, whereas you are giving guidance to the group on how they, with your help, can build a team and complete the task effectively.

PROMOTE DISCOVERY

We looked at this in Chapter 3. However, as a refresher and to develop a different perspective, I would ask you to look at Figure 6.1.

At the end of Chapter 4, we considered an integrated approach to vision, mission and values and made the point that the 'task', or left side, had to be integrated with the 'people', or right side.

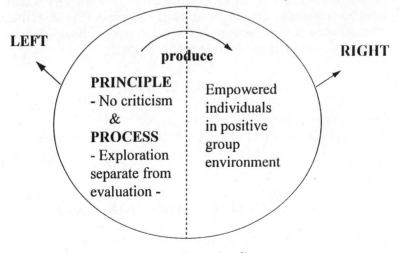

Figure 6.1 *Promoting discovery*

This shows how the integration is achieved – that you need to have determined the right principles and processes on the left side *in order to achieve* the creative and emotional freedom on the right side.

Provided you establish the principle of 'no criticism by word or body language' and the separation of exploration from evaluation, then the team and the individuals will achieve a high degree of creativity. Your role is to ensure that the principle and separation is followed, to explain why it is necessary, to create the right environment and then facilitate group discovery.

As we know this process is called brainstorming or group action thinking (GAT) and can be considered as a sub-process. In other words, GAT can be used whenever an open or discovery question is being considered, particularly What?, Why? and How?, as part of a complete process to achieve an objective like completing a team task.

A final point. You need to develop ideas or suggestions before evaluating them. Remember the case of the Alaskan Electricity Company? There needed to be focus of the entire group on the original suggestion 'why don't we shake the poles?' to produce the discovery of the helicopter solution. So encourage the development of ideas during the discovery process, and if that does not happen as a matter of course, pick some of the ideas that may be only half-formed and focus the group on developing them, with the no criticism rule still in place.

CREATE A TEAM VISION

I would draw your attention to Figure 6.2.

This process was set out in Chapter 2, and can be used as part of the final process, building a team, covered at the end of this chapter.

COMPLETE A TEAM TASK

Figure 6.3 focuses on a process to achieve a team task – the task process. It too is part of the wider process to build a team. The

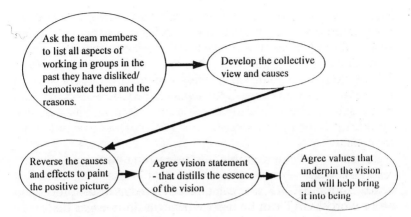

Figure 6.2 *A process to create a team vision and values*

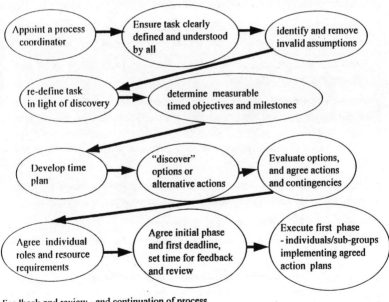

Feedback and review - and continuation of process

Figure 6.3 *Process to complete a team task*

actual steps and timing may well vary, according to the complexity and nature of the task the team faces. The actual process agreed should come in response to the question put to the team – what do we need to do to achieve the task successfully? However, by having a complete process provided in this book, you will be in a position to coach the team towards a process that you think will be effective. This process model can act as a benchmark, and is the development of the initial process set out in the first chapter.

Let us provide an example. Let us assume that you are made responsible for a small sales team – to develop business. This initial simple description of the task will need to be questioned and refined by the team. Some of the questions might be:

☞ QUESTIONS ☜

What sort of business – what is the specific product or service range we will focus on or will we aim to sell everything in our portfolio?

How will we ensure that we will sell business profitably – avoid the volume without profit trap?

What customers should we aim for? Should we focus on a specific type of customer to maximise penetration of product and profitability of sale? How can we qualify our leads to avoid getting customers we don't actually want or wasting time pursuing customers who are not serious about buying?

Should we focus on new business to new customers, or more business to existing customers, or different business to existing clients?

How do we help create satisfied customers?

From such questioning will come a more clearly defined and focused description of the task. For example:

☞ **ANSWER** ✍

Our task is twofold. One part is to provide perceived added value for a defined set of new strategic clients through profitable sale of a core range of financial products and services that will meet their needs. The other is to identify the strategic component of our existing client base and to increase their use of existing and new products and services, where it adds perceived value to them and profit to ourselves.

Once the hard bit is done – a clear, focused, but comprehensive description of the task – the rest of the process falls naturally into place.

RUN A SUCCESSFUL MEETING

This process was developed and implemented successfully in the workplace by a manager, Thomas, working for a financial services company.

Many meetings we attend as business people are not meetings of an intact team. They can be one-off meetings for a specific purpose (as was the case for Thomas – see the next paragraph for details) or irregular meetings (eg committees, working parties and steering groups), where the attendance varies so much (both in numbers and composition) that there is no consistency from one meeting to the next, and no real team. If we are 'in the chair', then we can adopt an approach and process which will maximise synergy rather than the 'negergy' that usually results. The process and approach Thomas adopted is set out in Figure 6.4.

The background was the follow-up to a company-wide staff attitude survey, where the head of the department had asked Thomas to manage the process for the department of around 70. There was a clear task objective.

He ran 11 peer-group meetings of between four and eight people, ie secretaries, clerks, officers, junior managers, middle

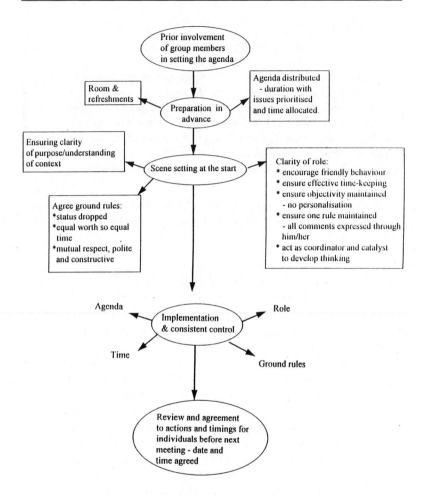

Figure 6.4 *Process for successful meeting*

managers, and one for the section heads (including his boss) and the head of department. The individual feedback from every meeting was that it was a success. Real issues had been raised and discussed, and effective solutions had been put forward. Invariably a positive, problem-solving atmosphere had been generated. Each individual left the meeting in the knowledge that his or her voice had been heard, and his or her ideas listened to. Ideas had been shared, common attitudes exposed and consensus solutions developed.

How was this achieved? There were six main factors – prior involvement, preparation, vision, clarity of role, ground rules, and consistent control. Looking at each in turn:

Prior involvement

Thomas decided to ignore the general findings of the survey, and ask every member of staff what they saw as the key issues. Because of the culture, there was no identification of individual response, simply classification by peer group. In this way, he ensured that at least one issue (and usually more, as many of the issues and problems were common) had been raised by each individual at the subsequent meetings to clarify matters and find solutions.

An agenda where all group members have contributed and feel involved has more impact and ownership than one determined purely by the leader.

Preparation

Thomas ensured a meeting room of the right size and equipment, near but not part of the department, ensured the creature comforts were catered for, and the agenda, with the issues prioritised and the length of the meeting, was sent out well in advance. Little things – but if the basics are not attended to, it can be difficult to have lift-off.

Vision

Thomas did not do much visioning as the context was clear, but he did preface every meeting with a few comments about how rare it was for members of staff to be involved in solving real work-related issues, how important it was for them to take full advantage, and how he hoped they would show enthusiasm and commitment.

Clarity of role

Thomas made it crystal clear what his role was and why. This helped manage expectations and generate certainty.

In this particular exercise he was a facilitator, meaning that he would:

❏ Encourage a friendly atmosphere.
❏ Ensure that objectivity was maintained, eg there was no degeneration into personalities/grievance or identifying individuals. Any 'personal' problem could be expressed in general terms.
❏ Ensure effective time-keeping.
❏ Ensure that one rule was maintained throughout the meeting, ie all comments should be expressed through the facilitator as this would avoid meetings within meetings or comments becoming too personal.
❏ Would not have any opinions himself (appropriate for a facilitator but not a teambuilder).
❏ Act as a catalyst to develop thinking where blind alleys or cul-de-sacs occurred.

Ground rules

In describing his role explicitly, Thomas set some ground rules. Additional ones he set out were:

❏ Status should be dropped.
❏ At this meeting, everyone had equal worth and so he would try to ensure they had equal time to express their views.
❏ He hoped that individuals would show mutual respect and any comments on other people's views would be polite and constructive.

At the end of the introduction, he asked if everyone was in agreement, and all verbally agreed, as it would have looked bad otherwise!

Consistent control

This gave Thomas the power to proceed according to the rules, and all he had to do was ensure they were kept.

It was certainly a novel approach to running a meeting, but Thomas told me that he had to try what was a culturally radical approach, because of the dimensions of the problems he knew he faced.

Most members of staff were sceptical and some were cynical. Being a large company, with years of success until the winds of change blew into a gale, it was still locked into a culture where behaviours accorded to established norms, based on hierarchy, status, conformity and the individual. Such environments are the breeding ground for scepticism and cynicism! Also, as the process was a first, there was a high degree of uncertainty and discomfort. There was a measure of resentment from his peers, seeing Thomas in a lead role, and his seniors did not want to be there!

His approach, as said earlier, was an outstanding success for all levels and all meetings. The key success factors that are transferable to any leader, running any meeting, and have relevance to teambuilding were:

❑ To set the objectives and ensure they were understood and agreed.
❑ To set expectations explicitly, gain agreement and ensure they were met.
❑ To set the rules of behaviour explicitly, gain agreement and ensure they were met.
❑ To ensure focus so that the business was completed on time.

For me, listening to his story, it reinforced the reality that if the ETB can create the right environment, he or she will get the response he or she and the task requires.

BUILD A TEAM

The four processes we have covered are essential components of the overall process to build a team – to become a better teambuilder.

The final section of this chapter looks at this process. There needs to be a starting point – we will assume that you are the ETB of a new team, so that you do not know the team-members. This is the first meeting, the objective of which is to start to build an effective team. You will need to change the process to fit your actual situation.

The moment has come. There you are in front of a group of people at 'confusion level'.

This is because it is a group meeting for the first time, a group expecting you to do something different, however positive it might be viewed. A change produces uncertainty and psychological discomfort, even if mixed with positive emotions as well.

So what are you going to do? You have all the power, and must have a clear idea of what you want to achieve and why at the first meeting. You must feel confident, as you will be the only one initially capable of operating at a high level of development.

Whatever you want to do, share it to start with. If your team knows early on what the objective of the meeting is, that will start removing the uncertainty straightaway. There will be a lot of silence initially – so don't let that throw you. You will get agreement, mainly with nods rather than words, to whatever you say is the objective!!

A final point before we proceed – be true to yourself and be honest. If it is an existing team you lead, and you have had an autocratic touch and are a pragmatic results-oriented individual (combining focusing and implementing), then play true to that reality. So perhaps an introduction along these lines would be appropriate.

> *Well, let's get started. Thanks, everyone, for being so punctual. You are probably wondering why you are here and what the purpose of this meeting is. Well it's simple. You know me, I like to make things happen and get results. And that's what this meeting is all about. I believe we'll get better results if we work better as a team. And that's what we're here for – to decide how we can improve teamworking, and agree an action plan by the end of the meeting. Is that OK?*

Universal 'agreement'.

Please refer to Figure 6.5. Let us look at each individual component of the process.

Acknowledge uncertainty

In the opening comments above, the embryonic ETB acknowledged uncertainty and 'agreed' the objective in his own style.

Style consistency is critical. The less-naturally team-oriented leader might, as an example, outline the process to build the team, achieve the task and gain verbal agreement, whereas the more team-oriented leader might involve the group in deciding the process. It doesn't actually matter.

The heart of teambuilding and synergy is 'effective problem solving' – whether the problem is the vision, task definition, or the process to achieve the task. Provided, at the first meeting, you act as facilitator of a brainstorming session, or ask someone to act

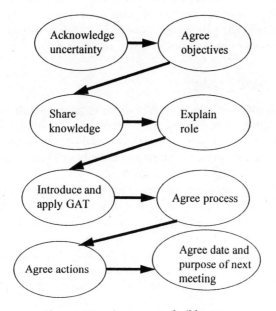

Figure 6.5 *A process to build a team*

as a facilitator (depending on your TSA preference), then things will work out, because the right behaviours in terms of questioning, listening and not criticising are being practised by all.

If you, the ETB, manage an act of effective discovery by the group at your first meeting, you will be setting the pattern of behaviour, which will generate success. You will also be proving to your team, whatever your particular style, that you mean what you say when it comes to improving team performance.

Agree the objective

Once everyone knows and understands why they are there, that will ease the tension visibly.

Share knowledge

You know much more about teams than anyone else present. So share your knowledge, eg the importance of process to teambuilding and task achievement, and how the team will decide together the right processes, how it is important that the team discovers and plays to its strengths and so on.

Explain your role

A key part of your role as ETB is to manage expectations. If they are not managed explicitly, then they will be set implicitly. If expectations are implicit, there is invariably a gap between leader and led, as many a poorly managed member of staff has found to their cost at the annual appraisal.

You will have an existing image in the eyes of your team if it is an already functioning unit. If not, the new team members will have formed ideas and expectations of a leader from their past experience and views of good leadership.

If you explain that your role is to help the building of an effective team, to manage an agreed process to achieve both the team goal and the task goal, and it is not to tell them what to do, that should go down like a breath of fresh air. You should also point out that there are always hiccups and crises dictated by living in a world of change, so there will be occasions when you will have to take control. That will also be understood and accepted, especially if you add that you will always explain the whys and wherefores.

Introduce and apply GAT technique

It is vital that only a small part of the meeting is devoted to your talking and the team listening. It is a necessary part of the meeting, as you need to talk and they want to listen. The more you ask questions, even if you do not get answers, the better. Within 15 minutes get into discovery mode. If GAT is a new technique, you will need to explain the principle and process, and perhaps practice on some silly issues to ensure that the right environment is created.

Then apply it to the question: 'What do we need to do to build an effective team?' That is better than asking: 'How do we build a better team?', as the former is more action-oriented – and ideas, as we know, are but alternative actions or areas for action.

Agree process

Out of this brainstorming should come the process to build the team. Remember, you are an active contributor whenever GAT is deployed – so you can put forward such things as developing a vision and values for the team, developing a clear definition of the task and the process to achieve it.

It is a good idea if you have a clear view, in advance of the meeting, of the process you want. Do not impose it, and be prepared to alter your views, but also be prepared to promote discovery, and, if necessary, suggest additions or subtractions. You know more about process and how teams develop than anyone else, so do not accept an inferior process for the sake of consensus.

If the team gets the process right, it will get the performance right. If it does not, it will not

We have already covered the processes to create a team vision, and complete a task. In terms of integration and order, as well as some additional items, suggestions would be:

❏ A social event for the team members only. Quoting Keith, the man brought in by the managing director of a glass manufacturing company (see Chapter 2, page 23) to build an effective team: *'It's very important when you start to develop a team that you understand your team members and what their capabilities are, what their limitations are, what their approach is, how they work, are they team people, are they individuals? How can they slot into a team? That was how I started – talking to people and getting to understand people, so that I can build on their strengths.'*

Now you have the team strengths audit to help identify and build on strengths – but a social/activity based setting will be a great help in getting to know your team, and should occur sooner rather than later in the teambuilding process.

❏ Collecting information – task and team.
❏ Sharing the information, including team strengths and implications of skill mix.
❏ Developing team vision.
❏ Developing task definition.
❏ Agreeing objectives and interim milestones.
❏ Brainstorming technical requirements, actions and timing.
❏ Completing a resources audit – agreeing budget, and who does what and when. Ensure roles are allocated, and play to strengths.
❏ Implementing first agreed phase, having agreed support, feedback and review mechanisms.

Agree actions

Before any meeting finishes, there should be a review of what has taken place, to confirm understanding. Then there should be agreement as to who is going to do what, why and when before the next meeting. These actions will be determined by progress along the task/team process. For example, one individual might organise a social event, another two might be collecting task-related information, you or someone else might be carrying out the team strengths audit, someone else looking at systems support, and the final member (could be you) writing up the minutes and putting forward a process model for consideration at the next meeting.

Agree time of next meeting and purpose

It may be that the team has agreed regular weekly meetings, in which case the next meeting is known. If not, it is sound policy to get the next meeting in everyone's diary before they leave, and for everyone to agree the objective for that meeting.

CONCLUSION

Your first meeting will be a triumph. It is the key to success. Subsequent meetings, assuming process is agreed, will be simply a matter of leading the process to a successful conclusion. Remember that, as the team grows in confidence and competence, you should build in feedback on individual performance, but not too soon. Such sessions must be handled with care, should only take place when there is consensus and should follow the two to one rule. What are the two things each individual is doing well and should develop further, and what is the one thing that could be improved.

It is a team session, preferably in an informal setting, and the starting point is not you, the leader, nor the other team members, but the individual himself or herself. We usually know best. So, *follow the 'promoting discovery' approach.*

If handled in the right way, such sessions are extremely powerful bonding devices that enable the team to help the individual grow and develop from a strong base.

However, we are not dealing with a static concept when it comes to the team, but a dynamic one. Your team will be subject to whole series of changes, all of which have the potential to diminish or destroy performance.

This is subject of the next chapter.

7

DEALING WITH CHANGE

INTRODUCTION

Change is a common denominator in all our lives today, and impacts on groups and group dynamics in much the same way as it impacts on the individual. As ETBs, we need to understand not only what levels teams pass through to performance, so that we can manage a smooth transition, but also how change can cause otherwise unexpected deterioration in performance.

To start with, we look at how individuals react to sudden change, perceived negatively, and, given that a team comprises individuals, consider how we should react as ETBs, when the team faces such changes.

Next we take a specific example of an ETB, in the role of coach and facilitator, helping a group of managers learn how to adjust to specific changes that teams face. To conclude, we consider the entire set of possible changes, the implications on the team and the strategies that the ETB needs to adopt to become a better teambuilder.

REACTION CURVE

Let us start by promoting discovery in you, the reader, rather than simply telling you the answer.

☞ **EXERCISE** ☜

I would like you to think back to an occasion when you experienced a change that was sudden, either in its announcement or in the occurrence, and which you perceived negatively.

Examples could be: receiving unexpected criticism in an area you thought yourself competent from someone whom you trusted and whose opinion you respected; being advised you were being made redundant; being told by a former partner that she or he was finishing the relationship – any change that was sudden, affected you personally and was perceived negatively.

Once you have recalled the change, take a pen and piece of paper and write down your feelings, thoughts and actions – but separated into three time-frames.

IMMEDIATE: the instant of the occurrence or announcement.

SHORT-TERM: hours and days after.

LONG-TERM: looking back after months or years.

If you could complete the exercise before carrying on reading, that would be very helpful, as otherwise there will be no discovery.

When I ask groups of managers to carry out this exercise, they invariably describe what is termed the transition or reaction curve. I would imagine that you will have done likewise. It is set out in Figure 7.1.

The initial reaction will be shock and disbelief, because the change is unexpected and makes zero connection with our current perception of reality. (Incidentally, that is why promoting discovery is such a psychologically powerful way of managing change for others. If, through the probing, effective and empathetic questioning of another, we gradually shift our perceptions until the moment of discovery for ourselves, we bypass the reaction curve completely as we will accept, believe in and become committed to changes we 'own' as a result of this process.)

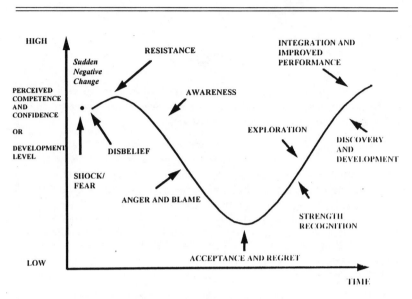

Figure 7.1 *The reaction curve*

However, where the change is sudden, externally announced or imposed, we will not make the transition from rejection to acceptance easily, perhaps not at all. If the change is traumatic, and we are not well developed, then disbelief may be permanent and conscious thought erase the memory of the incident.

A change like criticism tends to be unpleasant but not traumatic, so disbelief will be replaced by resistance, before dawning awareness and eventual acceptance. Interestingly, there can be a time when our perception of competence increases as we continue to resist. There was a production unit, whose workforce was told that it would be closed in six months and they would lose their jobs. For the first few weeks, they redoubled their efforts and denied the future reality.

Assuming we begin to recognise that we were not as good as we thought, then we start losing our confidence and feel much less competent. During this downward phase, we will tend to be full of emotions – anger, blame and regret, which are inevitable but counter-productive. The more extrovert we are, the more we will tend to blame others, particularly the source of the criticism, and the more introvert, the more we will blame and be angry with ourselves.

Eventually, we will accept the criticism to the extent we perceive it as valid. When we are at the nadir – at the bottom of the curve – we can get the balance wrong and perceive ourselves as less competent than we actually are.

Over time, there can and should be passage up the positive phase, when we begin to recognise that we are much more competent than we now think, where we explore and discover ways to improve competence, develop our skill and finally ensure improvement by integrating the best of the pre-change situation with the best of the new, eg we are more competent in the area criticised, we develop a more effective relationship with a new partner or we perform better in a new job and so on.

That is the theory, but the practice may be less than perfect, especially if we are too reliant on our own efforts and support mechanisms – if we do not challenge the change through assertive questioning or seek out others to help us through the change. This is another reason to believe in and build effective teams, because the power of the team guarantees effective support and learning for the individual.

Another crucial point is that criticism, invariably perceived negatively by the recipient, is a fundamentally flawed, inefficient and often ineffective development tool. Balanced feedback, initiated by the individual in a team context, is fundamental to effective learning and to the development of the individual.

Too often individuals criticise each other – nit-pick, find faults or blame for mistakes. If individuals criticise each other in teams, they will destroy the team. It is the function of an ETB to stop criticism in an immature team, but encourage feedback to create a mature one – reinforcing the point made in the previous chapter.

A final point to bear in mind is that, when an event comes as an unpleasant surprise to the team – and it inevitably will in a world of change – each individual member, including yourself, will automatically start descending down the reaction curve. ETBs, through prior knowledge, self-belief and confidence, have to recognise this reality for themselves and deal with it swiftly, eradicating the negative emotions and moving the team back to the commitment level.

Let us take an example.

A group of managers were trying to complete a two-day business simulation, as one of a number of teams.

This particular group had sailed through the early phases. They were carrying out the role of a subsidiary board running a pharmaceutical manufacturing company. The information had been digested and shared, the overall vision developed, a strategic plan devised, objectives set, and performance indicators and policies were in place.

They had to make quarterly decisions spanning three years, and had input into the computer the first two decisions. Delighted with the results, which exceeded expectations, the five were grouped together around the computer, having just input the third quarter's decision. They displayed all the hallmarks of a performing team – energy, commitment, focus, humour and very positive body language.

The results flashed up on the screen. Five pairs of eyes followed the screen down to the profit or loss for the quarter, not necessarily the sole yardstick for success, but one that all groups treat as king. They were expecting a modest profit. They saw a thumping great loss, in excess of £250,000.

Within less than a minute, the team had totally fragmented – descended from the commitment level to conflict in the twinkling of an eye. The managing director of the group told me in no uncertain terms what he thought of the simulation. He was an extrovert, quickly accepted the evidence of 'failure' and was allocating blame externally to the group. The personnel director disappeared to the toilet. The finance director went to a corner of the room, shaking his head in disbelief, clutching the printouts to his bosom. The production director and sales director entered a 'healthy dialogue', where each blamed the other for the debacle.

Now, assuming you were the teamleader or managing director, what should you do?

My suggestions would be:

1. Try to control your emotions. Until you are in control of

yourself, you have no hope of controlling the situation and building the team back to better performance. There is a simple technique to help you, which I call the *assertive pause*. This requires a deliberate act of pausing, using the power of the mind to stop the instinctive negative emotional response. This is followed by what is referred to as 'breathing through the rib-cage'. Normally we breathe shallowly at the top of the throats, which can lead, in moments of extreme stress, to hyperventilation. If we breathe slowly and deeply, taking the oxygen deep into the lungs, the oxygen is transferred to the brain – we literally clear our heads, enabling us to think more clearly, rationally and in a controlled way. This pausing and breathing deeply is a very effective technique to carry out at any times of stress or when we anticipate stress, eg just before an important meeting, presentation, interview and so on.

2. Call a review meeting.

3. Acknowledge the emotions that team members are feeling, point out the inevitable temporary fragmentation of the team – the descent to an overly individualistic and ego-centred state.

4. Suggest actions individuals or subgroups can take to review the data and consider the reasons behind the loss (or whatever the problem is). Emphasise the need to move away from blame and personalisation, however understandable that is.

5. Agree a meeting of the whole team in short order, where a team-based analysis of cause and effect can take place, using the base of research and thought that individuals and sub-groups have carried out.

6. At the meeting, lead the discovery of the cause or causes and agree the actions required to remedy the situation.

Now we turn to an ETB who is leading the discovery of some changes that occur in teams and how they should respond.

DISCOVERING THE IMPACT OF CHANGE

Background

Three teams of five managers had been operating in the outdoors on 'land' skis, ie two long thin planks of wood, with five equidistant holes in each plank, through which ropes passed, long enough to be held comfortably at shoulder height. Each set of two planks could accommodate a team of five managers, who stood with left feet on one plank and right feet on the other and tried to maximise the speed with which they moved forward on both planks. Their feet were not allowed on the ground.

After a series of runs with a formal leader or coach, each team had improved considerably. When they were instructed to proceed with no speaking allowed, each team's performance improved, much to everyone's surprise. However, when there was a switch in team members or team leader, there was a marked deterioration in performance. We take up the conversation, when the ETB is confirming two reasons why the performance improved, as the result of the imposition of silence.

Changing role of leader or builder

'Recapping', continued the ETB, 'we have discovered two reasons for the performance improvement. Firstly, the silence enabled focus on the feet, which moved the skis and secondly, the lack of noise and distraction not only enabled this focus to occur, but also changed a technical skill from conscious competence to instinctive learning. But there is a critical implication behind the result that we haven't yet uncovered. Can anyone think what it might be?'

'I know', said Peter emphatically. Everyone's attention instantly switched. 'It begs the question of the role of the leader. Here we have, right before our collective eyes, proven beyond doubt, an example of three teams who performed better without a leader than they would have done with one. Now that is interesting, is it not?'

'I have just been made redundant!' said George plaintively, and everyone laughed.

'It suggests, does it not, that the role of leader changes as teams develop', continued Peter. 'Once the leader has developed a mature team, united and focused on the task, then he or she needs no longer to lead from the front but the middle – to become one of the team rather than the teamleader.'

'All right in theory', said Tarisha, 'but difficult in practice, when our organisation appoints us to a teamleader role, and, I doubt, would not be very pleased if we gave it up.'

'I don't see that as a problem', Hermann suggested. 'We keep the title, and we retain responsibility for decision-taking, which will always be necessary if some crisis or change throws the team off course – but in terms of normal, effective performance, we become process facilitators rather than leaders, and even that role can switch between team members. In fact, I do that kind of thing myself. Team members take turns to chair meetings or run brainstorming sessions, and that works very well indeed.'

'Yes, that makes a lot of sense', agreed Tarisha, 'and helps develop all the team members' leadership skills. Yes, I will give that a go when I get back.'

Change in team membership

'OK', said the ETB. 'The next critical event was when I switched team members. Let us ask those who switched teams how they felt about that, first of all.'

'Well, a bit uncomfortable', said Tony, who had moved from Alison's team to Peter's. We hadn't much time to plan. And, as soon as I arrived, I was told by the leader what their approach was, and what the verbal instructions were, and what place I should take up, which was different from where I was accustomed, as I replaced the position vacated. I did my best in the run, though I made a few mistakes, and then went back to my own team with a hearty sigh of relief.'

'My feelings and experience were similar', said Harry, and Joanna also agreed. Joanna and Harry were the other two to have been displaced.

'And what was the result of this run?' asked the ETB.

'Well, performance deteriorated for all the teams, quite markedly', Alison replied.

'So what is the conclusion?' continued the ETB.

'If there is change in the composition of an effective team, the team performance will naturally deteriorate', came the quick reply from Tony.

'Agreed', said the ETB. 'Let us explore this a little bit further. Has anyone experienced a change in team composition in the recent past?'

'Yes, I have', said Joanna. 'I had a multinational team: two Americans, a Brit, a German and Dane. We had been together for nearly a year and had developed into a very supportive, cohesive and focused unit, producing some excellent results. One American was promoted and replaced by a Dutch guy, and things started to fall apart. At our first meeting, very much a strategic brainstorming affair, the Dutch guy almost had a stand-up fight with the British woman. I chatted with him afterwards, and he apologised, explaining that he profoundly disagreed with her views and felt he should express his own position. To cut a long story short, he never really settled in, and was sideways moved within a few months, much to the relief of the others, myself included, I am afraid to say.'

'And what, in your judgement, were the reasons for this unsuccessful outcome?' queried the ETB.

'First of all, I felt that I had been lacking in my leadership skills – I could have done better. Secondly, I thought there was just a personality clash: specifically that Hags had the wrong personality to fit into the team.'

'Anyone else got a recent experience to relate in this area?'

'Yes', said George. 'I too have a team, mostly American with one German and one Brit. It too developed into a united cohesive unit, and, also, one of the Americans was replaced with another, Jack. The problem was that the guy just wouldn't contribute in what had been a high octane, boisterous and busy environment. It was months before he started to actively contribute at team meetings – though now, to be fair, he is a fully integrated member.'

'Thanks, George', said the ETB. 'Let's see if we can draw some concrete conclusions. First of all, we know that any new member joining an unfamiliar group will feel uncomfortable, is not going to be confident and competent, and the team's performance will suffer. If you like, if you have an effective team which obeys D'Artagnan's motto "All for one and one for all", then once there is a replacement, that bond and the task focus is bound to be broken. To what extent do you see this as the consequence of individual personality – the personality of the stranger – and the clash with established group norms of behaviour?'

'It isn't primarily to do with personality, at all', replied Hermann excitedly. 'All our three new team members felt similarly, and all the teams' performance suffered. It is simply a function of group dynamics, if you like. The role personality plays is to determine the nature of the negative response, from a quarrel with Hags to opt-out with Jack.'

'So what is the learning for leaders, facing a replacement of one of their team members with another?'

'Go back to basics', suggested Zainol. 'Treat the entire team as if it was new. Re-build, re-generate the vision, reconsider task process, and re-create the bonding. As effective team leaders, we don't try to integrate a new member into an old team, which has died, we integrate all members, including the new one, into a new team, which lives.'

'That makes sense to me', agreed the ETB. 'What about everyone else?'

No-one disagreed.

Change in teamleader

'Before we move on, a final question. Imagine that there was an effective, united team from which one member left and you were the replacement. What is more, the member who left was the leader. You are the new teamleader.'

'I don't have to imagine', said Harry. 'Everything is starting to fit into place, you know. If we start at the theoretical level, the team members will be naturally inclined to reject their new leader, but they have to be careful, as he or she is their boss, with all the appraisal and other powers that position brings. So they are likely to resist, try to undermine his authority, say yes when they mean no and act according to their inclination rather than their word.

'They may well compare him behind his back very unfavourably with the old leader, whom they respected and who represented the happy past. From the leader's perspective, he won't know exactly what is going on, but will find himself thwarted and frustrated, will find the changes he wants are not implemented when he wants or as well as he expects. He may well begin to dislike specific individuals, and be inclined to move more and more into command and control, as his attempts at a more open involving approach seem to have failed. That's the theory and my experience in the recent past.'

'And there will be variations on that theme for all new leaders', continued Tarisha, 'again not because of personality, but the power of group dynamics.'

'So what should effective leaders do in this situation?' asked Chew rhetorically. 'I know', he continued. 'Look, listen and learn, and then start to build a new team from scratch.'

ALL THE CHANGES

In this final section, we consider all the possible changes that can occur to upset the team you have built into a high performing unit. We then look at what needs to be done to stop the team falling back to conflict level or to restore it back to commitment, when descent down a level or two cannot be avoided.

You may have noticed the phrase in the last paragraph 'what needs to be done', and not 'what you need to do'. One reality of a performing team is that every team member develops into a potential teamleader.

In fact a good ETB will have deliberately helped team members achieve this result, whether by alternating the facilitation of the brainstorming sessions, or the co-ordination of the agreed process at team meetings.

Now your particular style or the reality of positional power in a hierarchy may mean that you retain control of the process and step in to take charge of the team's recovery from the impact of change. Whatever the case may be, it would be wise to ensure that each team member is aware of what needs to be done and why – because there will be times when you are not there.

Let us start by looking at Figure 7.2. We will look at each change in turn.

The unexpected

In achieving any task, project, milestone or mission, the unexpected will inevitably occur. That is the consequence of operating in a world of change. By agreeing and applying an effective teambuilding and task achievement process, you reduce the probability of such events, but you cannot eliminate them.

These days, the unexpected is rarely good news! If it is, there is no problem. Individuals and teams tend to take good news in their stride. Having said that, the unexpected, even if good news, produces uncertainty and it is sound policy to hold a review meeting to ensure the good news is shared, the consequences appreciated and any alterations in timetables or process carried out.

Regular communication between all team members is an integral part of teambuilding and maintenance of focus and performance. It is even more important, if the news is bad. The unexpected can happen, when the team is performing together. Remember the group of executives who were succeeding at the business simulation, and degenerated rapidly into conflict when they made a significant and unexpected loss – triggering off descent down the reaction curve for each individual.

In the work situation, that is not often the case, as teams rarely carry out implementation of strategy as a single unit. Implementation tends to occur through individuals and subgroups carrying out agreed roles. Strategy formulation and review of implementation is the focus of team-based activity.

The unexpected tends to occur as the result of external circumstances beyond the team's control, advised to you as ETB, or it occurs to individuals implementing strategy. For instance, a budget can be slashed by head office or the parent company, a deadline brought forward by a demanding client, a delivery date

CHANGE	Impact on stage of development of team	STRATEGIC RESPONSE BY ETB
Unexpected	*Conflict*	* Review meeting * Refocus on problem-solving
Varying team membership	*Co-operation, then conflict*	* Attendance rule * Clear communication to and from missing team members
Permanent departure of team member	*Co-operation, then conflict*	* Review meeting * New task process * Re-prioritisation team/individual work * Expand areas for team-working
Replacement of team member	*Conflict*	* Back to teambuilding, as if all team were new
Task completed/ new task	*Conflict*	* New task process

Figure 7.2 *Changes affecting team performance*

for an important resource such as an IT system postponed.

Where you are the conduit of the bad external news, it is important that you hold a meeting to review the impact and brainstorm the way forward.

The internally generated bad news causes more problems – especially if your team has not yet fully matured. We are talking about what could be viewed as 'mistakes', perceived as attributable to individuals who 'cause' them, leading to rapid deterioration of the team to conflict level as blame creeps in and personalities start clashing.

This is where your role as teambuilder becomes critical. You need to manage expectations, and agree positive ground rules for individual team members early on in the teambuilding process.

As you know, mistakes will be made (and you will make them as well). The rule that should be impressed on every team member is that, if any 'errors' are not time-critical, they should be brought up at the regular team review of progress and process.

If time critical, each team member is empowered to call a review meeting, so that the problem is discussed and solved. You should definitely lead by example, and perhaps even create an example early on!

Otherwise, the natural tendency will be to cover them up, which will compound the problems over time for the effectiveness of task completion, for the individual concerned and hence for the team's ability to perform.

Alternatively, the individual will come to you as the ETB. This might sound fine, as no doubt the two of you can solve the problem, but is against the interest of the team as a whole. It breaks the rule of open, team-based communication, can lead to a perception of individual favouritism, and so builds up a head of steam, counter to the overall dynamics of a commitment team. The kettle will eventually boil over.

This also explains the importance of identifying and playing to strengths, not weaknesses, and the power of process, specifically identifying where there is need for technical competence beyond current team capability.

Teams should stretch individuals. This means individuals will be learning new skills in order to complete the project or accomplish the task. Mistakes, 'the stepping stones to success', are inevitable when we learn. If it is recognised that they are inevitable, there is a much greater chance that, when they occur, they are only unexpected as to timing and are treated by team-members as an opportunity to help a colleague learn, and a problem-solving rather than fault-finding exercise.

Varying membership at meetings

Most people do what they want to do, if they can get away with it. We focus on doing what is important to us. This may well not accord with what is the right priority to achieve the task effectively. We often spend lots of time doing things we like, and avoid unpleasant tasks that we know we should do, but can never quite find the time to address!

The more variation in membership at team meetings, the less chance of building or maintaining a performing unit.

It is important, therefore, that you stress the need for every individual to place the highest possible priority on attending agreed meetings, and ensure that you set an example. There is a virtuous circle prevailing as well. If you are effective at the first meeting, team members will want to attend the second, and so they will.

However, the reality of hectic business life, when we have to do a host of tasks not related to the team we work for, and have to deal with the unexpected on a regular basis, means that there will be occasions when we will miss a meeting.

You will find that, as an ETB, these occasions will be rare, and not the norm. The way to deal with them is to ensure you or the designated co-ordinator, if it is you that is absent, receive a full briefing of progress by any absentee beforehand, preferably face-to-face, which is shared and discussed at the meeting. Equally, the absentee should be fully advised of the decisions taken at the meeting, including those that involve him or her in additional work! Consent should be obtained after the event by explaining the whys and wherefores.

Permanent departure of team member

These are the days of cost-cutting, where most managers have to achieve more with less – to work smarter rather than harder. Now the team is the smartest way there is to work. That has been one key message of the book and will be a reality for you, when you have built an effective team.

However, it does happen that an existing team – whether board, departmental, functional or project has one of its members permanently removed, rather than replaced, because of a structural or cost-cutting exercise.

This will put enormous strain on the team. There will be a gradual descent to the co-operation level, as the group has bonded and can adjust easily to the absence of a friend rather than the presence of a stranger (replacement). But, in the absence of effective intervention by the ETB or designated co-ordinator, unplanned increase in work on the individual will lead to the conflict level, both from the extra stress and strain of extra duties in an already busy life, and the probable development of conflict between individuals, where one is doing more than another and feels unfairly treated.

Clearly there needs to be a team meeting to take a fresh look at the task process, and ensure that the additional work falling on the team is allocated fairly. This will usually mean a transference of tasks between team members as well as the re-allocation of tasks previously carried out by the dearly departed. The chances are that one or two individuals will have the appropriate technical skills or technical base to absorb the majority of tasks allocated. Unless they lose some of their existing workload to other team members, then they will perceive themselves as being unfairly treated.

All that is not sufficient, because something else or a combination of something elses must also happen. Most people I know work hard and put in long hours. If all need to work even harder and longer, there will be too much stress on the team.

So ways need to be found to ensure that overall hours worked do not increase. Suggestions would be, and they are not exclusive:

1. Consider dropping the least important work – the stuff that really does not need to get done by the team. In other words carry out a re-prioritising exercise, to gain greater focus on activities that are core to the team.
2. Extend this re-prioritisation to the work the individual does, unrelated to the team – we all have individual responsibilities as well as work emanating from team membership. This will enable the individual to identify the relatively trivial and eliminate it.
3. Use the opportunity to see if there cannot be a greater simplification of process, enabling the team and the individual to work smarter rather than harder.
4. If not already the case, suggest a new rule as regards the tasks that individuals carry out separately from the team. This is simply that individuals can and should hold quick and dirty brainstorms involving the team as a whole to help with the scoping of the task, and the formulation and implementation of the strategy to achieve the task. This will increase the quality and quantity of individual output, so reducing the time individuals take to complete their tasks.

REPLACEMENT OF TEAM MEMBER

This is the single greatest cause of the permanent breakdown of a previously performing team – because a friend departs and a stranger arrives.

We looked at this briefly earlier in the chapter, when the ETB reviewed the ski exercise. What happens, when there is no understanding and no ETB, is that the poor innocent replacement is forced to become the friend that has been lost!

This never works and so leads to breakdown. The reason this happens is quite easy to comprehend. The team, which has bonded, grieves the loss of a friend and resents the arrival of a stranger – human nature. That is an understandable and emotional response. There is an inevitable urge to close ranks against the impostor, whatever kind and false words have been spoken to the new member.

The only way the stranger can become accepted is if he or she becomes the friend they have lost. So there is enormous pressure at the psychological level to get the 'new colleague' to conform to the unwritten rules or norms of behaviour the team has developed. The individual is expected to be a mature, developed team member with the same set of skills and personality as the departed team member!

This will hardly ever be the case.

As an aside, this reality is why a number of companies, which have achieved a team-based culture, have as a necessary consequence the rule that the team hires the replacement!

That does not help you, unless you have the power to recruit and have involved the team in the decision. And even if the new member has a similar set of skills and strengths as the member who has left, he or she will still be coming in at confusion level and will not share the team vision and values, as they were not part of the visioning process.

This is why you have to go back to the beginning and restart the team building process, as if all the team were new!

This is not, in fact, a time-consuming process, and acts as a refresher for the existing team members, enabling a renewal of motivation and often fresh discovery as the new team member will contribute new insights and perspectives, as she is able to share experience in a positive environment.

When it comes to task process, it will often be the case that the strengths audit indicates a set of preferences which differ in some degree from the team member who has left. Also the technical competence may be different. This means a redefining of roles and perhaps a shuffling of tasks across the team, so that any holes are plugged, and new development paths involving existing team members as well as the new member identified and agreed.

It is worth pausing to consider in more depth the case when the new member is the ETB. Hitherto, we have examined the situations where you become the ETB of a new team, or are the leader of an existing group, which you have decided to build into an effective team.

Often in your career, you will replace another teambuilder and be the stranger among friends!

On a development programme, when this issue emerged, the consensus advice was to do nothing! In other words, spend a few weeks in questioning and listening mode (as suggested by Chew on page 104), reacting sympathetically to any comments about the old boss (which are not always favourable, if you are in the fortunate position of replacing a tyrant). By behaving as an ETB from the start, and explicitly acknowledging that your predecessor was one of the best, as is the team you are now in charge of, you overcome the fears and concerns and sense of loss of the team, gain respect as you exceed expectations held in advance and prepare a very firm base on which to build your team.

Achieving the task

Some teams, eg project teams, have a defined duration. Once the project is finished, the team is disbanded. If you are the ETB, then ensure that success is fully celebrated, hold a final meeting to agree whether the team should meet again and when to swap notes, and suggest individuals develop an action plan to use their expanded network in the future.

However, many teams are 'eternal' or at least long term – such as departmental teams, business unit teams, functional teams, board teams and so on.

There will be shorter-term goals and objectives, often of an annual nature, which will become the focus for such teams. Once these are achieved the teams become vulnerable. I have seen this both inside organisations and also when developing teams. The team works out the right process to achieve a given task, succeeds and celebrates. It then moves on to another task and promptly fails. From commitment to conflict in the twinkling of an eye. The reason is twofold:

1. The task requires a different process for success to be achieved. The team applies the process that succeeded before.
2. The task requires new roles and a new set of technical skills. The team applies the same roles and the same set of technical

skills, which achieved success. Individuals fail, and then the team fails.

That is why the ETB should take the team back to the beginning of the task process, though not the teambuilding process, for any new project, task or mission.

Finally, teams succeed through the stretch provided to the individuals. Individuals in successful teams become hungry to learn, to be stretched more and to achieve more.

This means that the horizons of the team need to expand and you, as ETB, need to ensure that the tasks selected are progressively more difficult, demanding and hence fulfilling.

Giving a team tasks well within current capability is just as likely to produce the conflict level as giving the team a stretching task and not ensuring that a new task process is agreed and technical skills developed.

QUESTIONING ASSUMPTIONS: SOME ANSWERS

I have put first an answer based on a specific assumption and then some other answers that groups have come up with, based on other assumptions, shown in brackets.

☞ ANSWERS ☜

1. She cannot count (a Siamese twin, a toy, a pet, a pregnant mother, a corpse floating by).

2. Run over by car, as he is blind and sold his guide-dog. (Mugged on the way home as it was a very valuable dog; killed by his wife as it was, for this group, her dog; fallen down a crevasse, as he was an Eskimo and sold his husky.)

3. Climbed a block of ice, which melted.

4. Playing monopoly: toy car and hotel.

5. Triangular pyramid or tetrahedron, ie three in an equilateral triangle and one on the top of a hill or bottom of a hole. This problem cannot be solved if we assume we have to operate in two dimensions. I learnt this problem years ago and was told by the tutor that one of his colleagues was a rather arrogant individual and let a group of managers sweat on this for 15 minutes until one member (very strong in focusing) came up to him and hit him, crying, 'How dare you waste my time on a problem to which there is no solution'.

6. No navels. This is an example of the power of visualisation to increase creativity.

7. There can be all sorts of stories from the ribald (plucked from celebrating the post mile-high club by sudden decompression) to the ridiculous. The best (again breaking out of two dimensions) is the hot-air balloon with two men in it, losing height and getting closer to the hills. Throwing all the equipment out is not sufficient, throwing out all the clothes doesn't do the trick either – but the ultimate sacrifice does. The man with the short straw jumps out and the balloon, with its sole occupant, ascends to safety.

REVIEW

In this final chapter, we review the key messages from the earlier chapters, to act as an *aide-mémoire*, as well as providing space for you to produce your personal action plan to become a better teambuilder.

1. Voyage of discovery

This chapter introduced key themes and finished with a case study. The 'blindfold squares' exercise highlighted the behaviour of immature groups – specifically:

❑ Too much talking, and not enough listening – vying for leadership.
❑ The one with the first idea that is accepted becomes the leader, but that can change if someone else takes over development or implementation.
❑ The group becomes locked into the 'one right answer' and alternatives are dismissed.
❑ Followers can become committed to the task, but don't really understand it and so implement it badly.
❑ Sub-grouping with little cross-communication.
❑ Individuals becoming very dogmatic.
❑ People only really comfortable with a lot of action, even though there has been little thought.
❑ Satisfaction with the solution until the group realises it is inferior or inadequate, after they have finished.

Many of these behaviours are demonstrated by immature groups in the workplace.

The effective group was led by an effective team builder (ETB), who applied and controlled a process to optimise task achievement. He or she had been given the specific role of process co-ordinator, and made sure that the group did the right things in the right order.

The initial process followed was:

1. Appoint a process co-ordinator.
2. Ensure task clearly defined and understood by all.
3. Identify and remove invalid assumptions – redefining the task.
4. Develop options for task completion.

Other key requirements identified at this stage for an ETB were to have:

❏ Good questioning and listening skills to be able to promote discovery in the group, rather than just telling them what to do.
❏ Identified the strengths of the individuals and, in the early stages of building the team, played to those strengths to build competence and confidence.
❏ Learnt how to deal with all the changes the team will face.

The case study was told in the words of the teamleader Glyn Murphy, who led a multi-skilled unit operating in a Health Authority.

Key new messages derived were:

❏ Effective teams agree vision, mission and strategy as a team. Implementation is necessarily carried out on a sub-group or individual basis. Regular team communication ensured the sharing of experience and team support to solve individual problems.
❏ Effective teambuilding may require an off-site event, but part of any such event should focus on work issues.
❏ Effective brainstorming is the key technique to build the team and complete the task.
❏ Effective teams become self-managing units. They need freedom to breathe and to be stretched by more demanding and difficult tasks.

2. The effective team

Here we considered answers to four questions: 'Why build a team?', 'What does an effective team look like?', 'What are the barriers to achieving success?', and 'How can they be overcome?'.

Why build a team?

Research cites such important benefits for organisations as improvement in productivity, quality, job satisfaction, and customer satisfaction, reduction in waste and the increased ability for team members to resolve their own disputes.

For the individual, the effective team is the most powerful development tool for all the individual members, including the ETB.

What does an effective team look like?

By reversing all the negative factors of working in immature groups, a vision of an effective team was produced. Key components were:

❏ A cleared, shared sense of direction and purpose.
❏ Enthusiastic, committed team members, who are all involved and participate.
❏ A focus on achieving stretching and demanding tasks and goals.
❏ Humour, enjoyment and learning.
❏ Mutual support and helping each other develop and grow individual strengths.
❏ The capacity for individuals to be assertive and challenge and explore issues raised by others in order to generate better solutions.
❏ Good listening skills as well as good questioning skills.

The core values suggested were openness, honesty, mutual respect, trust, sharing and humour.

What are the barriers and how can they be overcome?

Key organisational barriers are the attitudes of top decision-makers, which can be hostile; too much focus on achieving tasks; a lack of strategic thinking skills; a hierarchical structure with positional power and downward appraisal; and systems which reward individual and not team performances.

Whatever the organisational barriers, being in a leadership position provides any leader with the potential to build an effective team, as was demonstrated in what could be considered a very hostile corporate environment.

Individual barriers consist of lack of belief in a team by the team-leader; insufficient skills or the wrong mix among team-members; physical separation of the team; and too many people in the team.

The individual barriers can only be removed by recognising that becoming a better teambuilder is, in fact, easy. The 'questioning assumptions' exercise was aimed at demonstrating how easy it is to create the right environment to promote discovery by the group. If a group can discover through the quality of questioning and listening skills in a defined process, then it will generate synergy (the whole being greater than the sum of the parts), and not the usual 'negergy'.

3. Promoting discovery

The core skills of effective questioning and listening, creative thinking and the powerful teambuilding technique of brainstorming or group action thinking (GAT) which are vital to the promotion of discovery by the team, were considered.

The need to ask open, probing questions using 'what, how, why' was demonstrated with the Alaskan Electricity example. The importance of developing listening skills, the use of positive body language and feedback were demonstrated.

Key points on creative thinking were: to recognise that ideas could be viewed from a pragmatic basis – merely areas for action or alternative action; that it was important to be objective and to uncover and remove false assumptions that closed our minds down; and that brainstorming or GAT was a very powerful technique to ensure the free flow of ideas and help build the team.

It was critically important that exploration of alternatives should be separated from evaluation and judgement. The golden rule, which needed to be understood before introducing GAT and applied during it, was that there must be no criticism by word or body language. If this rule was followed, then not only would there be group discovery, but every individual would become more creative. 'The more logical we are, the more creative we can be.'

4. How groups behave

Here we looked at the individuals' and the groups' stages or levels of development, and concluded with the interaction between individuals, the task and the group and what the ETB needed to do to produce a commitment level team.

Individuals demonstrate different behaviours, depending on whether they are striving for *security*, building *self-esteem*, or operating at the highest level – the *growth* level. When striving to gain security we are very self-centred, striving to control our environments and, if we are leaders, our followers. As we build our self-esteem, we tend to be individualistic and achievement oriented – proving to ourselves how good we are. Only when we have developed an inner strength, and feel confident and competent in our humanity and our abilities, can we develop an effective focus on others – whether team members or customers.

These levels of individual development translate to stages or phases of team development, with the six Cs: confusion, when the group first met, leading to conflict or with a strong visionary leader to control, where team members are immature instruments of the leader's vision. A higher level of development was demonstrated by the co-operation phase, but in the absence of a drive to achieve the team's tasks this could degenerate into consensus, where the team members were very comfortable with each other, but more socially oriented than task oriented, with little challenge and hence discovery in the group.

The highest level corresponding to the individual *growth* level was the commitment level – the effective or high-performance team.

There are three factors that needed to be addressed if the team was going to be built. These were the requirements of the task, the needs of the individual, and the dynamics of the group. The key requirement of the ETB was to generate alignment between the three, and use the power of vision, mission, and process to create that alignment.

The mission answered the questions of what the team was going to achieve as its ultimate goal by when. It was important that success should be measurable, and that there was clear process to achieve the *task*. Vision and associated values were people-focused, and answered the 'why' and 'how' questions.

5. The team mix

Team-members' strengths can be identified using a simple questionnaire, the Team Strengths Audit or TSA, which asks the individual to prioritise his or her preferences when working in a team. The eight strengths are investigating, innovating, evaluating, focusing, implementing, finishing, supporting and co-ordinating.

If all are present without duplication in the team, this gives the greatest potential for effective performance. Any missing strengths would need to be developed, and duplications, particularly focusing, where there was potential for personality clashes, would need to be resolved by the team.

6. The power of process

This was a very pragmatic chapter and examined the following five processes:

1. Promoting discovery
2. Creating a team vision and values
3. Completing a team task
4. Running a successful meeting
5. Building a team.

These five processes were summarised in Figures 6.1–5.

7. Dealing with change

This chapter looked at how individuals reacted to sudden change perceived negatively, and its impact on the team, then demonstrated how an ETB produced discovery of the impact of key changes that teams experienced. It concluded with the complete set of changes that can occur and the strategies that the ETB should adopt to maximise the possibility of positive outcomes.

When individuals experience sudden change perceived negatively, there is a downward emotional spiral, with shock and resistance, if not initial rejection, followed by anger and blame on the way to acceptance. Self-esteem is reduced in the negative phase. Subsequently, there will be an objective recognition of strength and the exploration and discovery of new ways to produce a higher level of perceived and actual competence, than was the case when the sudden change took place.

The relevance to teambuilding is that the ETB needs to be aware of the impact of the *unexpected*, which is perceived negatively; must first personally break out of the downward curve through using the 'assertive pause' and then help the team by calling a meeting to acknowledge the emotional reality and help move the group into a positive problem-solving mode and away from the negative mode of individual criticism and scapegoating.

It was important that everyone made attendance at team meetings a top priority. If there was *varying membership*, it was vital that there was clear communication to and from absent members before and after the meeting.

If one team member *left without replacement*, initially the team would drop to the co-operation level, and then to conflict due to extra pressure put on individuals and a perception that some had suffered more than others, when it came to the sharing of duties.

There should be a meeting to review the task process, and ensure that there was a shift in workflows of individuals and subgroups, which accorded to competence and was perceived as fair.

In order to reduce the burden of the loss, re-prioritisation should take place of individual workflows to eradicate the least important, and/or the GAT technique extended to work by individuals outside the team-allocated work to enable the individuals to work smarter.

When one team member left and was *replaced by a new team member*, it should be recognised that there would be a natural and strong pressure for the new member to conform to the existing group norms, with he or she likely to be resented as an inferior substitute of a friend who had left.

As a result, it was necessary to recommence the teambuilding process from scratch as if all the existing members were new.

Finally, the greatest moment of vulnerability of the team was when it had *achieved its particular mission, task or goal*. Assuming the team was not to be broken up, then the next mission should be determined and a new process agreed and implemented. If the team carried on to the next task on a wave of euphoria without a new process, there was a high probability that unexpected mistakes would be made as the new mission demanded different technical skills and different roles agreed for individuals and sub-groups.

This would lead to descent to the conflict level.

ACTION

This is an opportunity for you to pause and plan before building a better team, hence becoming a better teambuilder or ETB.

To help you, I will ask a few questions. I assume that you have a group of staff, where you have the positional power of leader or have been given authority by the group itself to be the teambuilder.

Yourself

❑ How confident are you in your abilities to be an ETB, on a scale of 1 (low) to 6 (high)?

❑ Do you feel the need to experiment before developing your skills with your actual workteam?

❑ If so, did you carry out the 'Questioning Assumptions' with your workteam. If so, what was the result? If not as good as you hoped, what do you think were the reasons, and what can you do to improve the situation?

Note If you have not, you may want to kick off the team-building process at a special, fun meeting where you oversee the exercises and have as a workgoal the successful implementation of the GAT technique.

Have you completed the TSA yourself? If you have, how do your preferences impact on your ability to be an ETB, particularly to co-ordinate process and not just push for task completion?

Your team members

Assuming, which is likely, that you have met some or all of your team – in fact may well have been working with them for a while:

❑ What would your guesses be as to each member's top two preferred team strengths?
❑ Assuming, which is highly likely, that you like some better than others, you may even have a favourite and a 'black sheep', does comparison with your estimate of their top two preferences and your own preferences give any clues as to those feelings?

The team

❑ At what stage of development would you say your team is now and why?

The task

❑ How clearly defined is the overall mission and are there quantifiable objectives/milestones?
❑ How variable is the performance of different individuals in the team, and to what extent is any variability a function of lack of a commitment level team or individual technical competence?

The strategy

There are a number of choices:

1. Additional action by you before calling a meeting with the objective of building a better team, eg carrying out the 'Questioning Assumptions' exercise to create a good environment, giving them all a copy of this book (sharing knowledge) to read and then calling a meeting to share the TSA results and consider how to proceed, or giving them all the TSA to complete and calling a meeting to determine team mix and implications.

2. Holding the first meeting with the objective of building a better team, in which case you will need to decide:

❑ How to manage expectations – how and what you will communicate before the event takes place.
❑ What you want the team to have achieved by the end of that meeting.
❑ What process or processes you need to adopt to ensure the objective is achieved?

In summary, you may like to complete a simple action plan – the first few actions you intend to take, the reason and the timing.

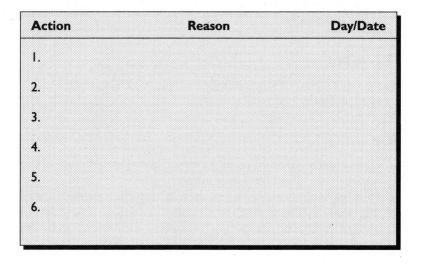

Action	Reason	Day/Date
1.		
2.		
3.		
4.		
5.		
6.		

Final words

In conclusion, if I were asked to focus on the three vital ingredients to becoming a better teambuilder, they would be:

1. Use GAT to create the environment.
2. Use process to build the team.
3. Use humour to maximise fun and learning.

RECOMMENDED READING

Adair, J (1988) *Effective Leadership*, Pan, London.

Belbin, Meredith R (1981) *Management Teams: Why They Succeed or Fail*, Butterworth-Heinemann, Oxford.

Bennis, W (1989) *On Becoming a Leader*, Addison-Wesley Publishing Company, USA.

Blanchard, K and Johnson, S (1983) *The One Minute Manager*, Fontana, London.

De Bono, E (1982) *Lateral Thinking for Management*, Penguin, London.

Eales-White, R (1992) *The Power of Persuasion: Improving Your Performance and Leadership Skills*, Kogan Page, London.

Eales-White, R (1994) *Creating Growth from Change: How You React, Develop and Grow*, McGraw-Hill, Maidenhead.

Eales-White, R (1995) *Building Your Team*, Kogan Page, London.

Harrison, R (1991) *Humanizing Change: a Culture-Based Approach*, Harrison Associates, USA.

Herrmann, N (1988) *The Creative Brain*, Brain Books, Lace Lure, North Carolina, USA.

Mackay, I (1984) *A Guide to Listening*, Bacie, London.

Marguerison, C, and McCann R (1990) *Team Management: Practical New Approaches*, WH Allen & Co, London.

Montebello, A and Buzzotta, V (1993) 'Work Teams that Work', *Training and Development Journal*, March 1993, American Society for Training and Development Inc, Alexandra, USA.

Pease, A (1981) *Body Language: How to Read Others' Thoughts by Their Gestures*, Sheldon Press, London.

Peters, T (1987) *Thriving on Chaos, Handbook for a Management Revolution*, Knopf, New York.

Rosen, N (1989) *Teamwork and the Bottom Line: Groups Make a Difference*, Lawrence Erlbaum Associates, Hillsdale, New Jersey, USA.

Shaw, M (1981) *Group Dynamics, The Psychology of Small Group Behaviour*, McGraw-Hill, Maidenhead.

Van Maurik, J (1994) *Discovering the Leader in You*, McGraw-Hill, Maidenhead.

Zenger, J, Musselwhite, E, Hudson K, and Perrion, C (1991) 'Leadership in a Team Environment', *Training and Development*, USA.

INDEX